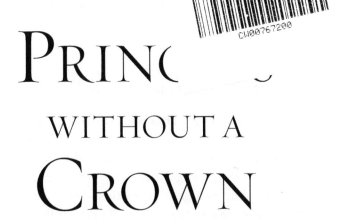

PRINC

WITHOUT A

CROWN

Returning to My Jewish Roots

JENNA MAIO

ISBN: 978-965-7041-20-8 (hardcover)
ISBN: 978-965-7041-21-5 (paperback)
ISBN: 978-965-7041-22-2 (e-book)

Publishing services provided by JewishSelfPublishing. The author acts as the publisher and is solely responsible for the content of this book, which does not necessarily reflect the opinions of JewishSelfPublishing.

www.jewishselfpublishing.com
info@jewishselfpublishing.com
(800) 613-9430

The author can be contacted at at jenna@modernjewishgirl.com.

We sincerely hope you enjoy reading this book. The author would be very gratified if you would show your support by posting a nice review.

This book is dedicated to:

My grandma Bea and my parents, Jaime and Paul,
for always believing in me and supporting me.

My brother, Mark, for giving me the push I needed
to publish this book.

And to my husband, Justin, who encourages me
to pursue my dreams every day and without whom
this book would never have happened.

I love you all.

In memory of

My great-grandmother, Faigel Rochel (Fanny) Steinfeld

And my grandparents, Henry and Hortense Shweitzer

This book should be an aliyah for their neshamos.

"From the straits I called upon G-d,
He answered me with expansiveness."

— *Psalms 118:5*

Contents

PART I
INSPIRATION

PART II
STRUGGLE

PART III
TRANSCENDENCE

Preface

ALTHOUGH I GREW UP IN the Five Towns, I did not know a single religious Jew. We initially lived in my father's childhood home in Woodmere Park, but when my secular parents realized that "the Orthodox" were closing in on us, we moved to Hewlett Harbor. (It's ironic that we would intentionally leave a religious community, only for me to find my way back to it years later!)

I remember driving in the car when I was about seven years old and my parents saying that I wasn't going to have many friends if we stayed in Woodmere because "the religious" wouldn't let their kids play with me. "They took over," I heard again and again, as my parents went on to mourn a town that was no more. Cedarhurst, the shopping center, once a hub for teenagers to shop and hang out and go to the movies on Saturdays, became a ghost town on Saturday, locked up for Shabbos. Today the movie theater and diner are no more; the street is lined with kosher restaurants and wig shops.

Religious day school wasn't an option, and the Lawrence public schools in our district were suffering because more and more kids were attending yeshivah instead. So off we went to Hewlett, where we could stay safe in our secular Jewish bubble. I went to public school, and although most of my friends were Jewish, we were all pretty clueless about Judaism. We quietly mocked Orthodox people in the street ("Why won't they join the twenty-first century?!") and I got kicked out of Hebrew school.

For the first two years of college, I did not step foot into Chabad or Hillel. Based on my superficial Hebrew school education, I naively thought, like many American Jews, that Judaism was an outdated religion filled with arbitrary rituals.

I was shocked to discover, at age nineteen, that Judaism was deep and relevant, filled with meaning behind every custom. And although I had questions — lots of them — it became clear pretty quickly that the Torah is a holy and Divine text.

When I first began to learn Torah and observe the mitzvot, commandments, it was like experiencing the world as a child again. It was all so new and exciting. This phase is what Rabbi Akiva Tatz calls "Initial Inspiration."* It's like falling in love.

As the years went on, my childlike vision faded away and "real life" resumed. I struggled to make time to learn Torah in law school. It was difficult to keep growing in my observance in the face of challenges from family and friends. I was constantly on the defense while trying to stay inspired. This, Rabbi Tatz explains, is the second phase in any growth process, the "Struggle." The struggle is real.

Now, as a religious wife and mother, I have made Torah observance my own. My family and friends accept that I am religious. I'm doing my best to run a Torah home. I have achieved what Rabbi Tatz calls "Transcendence."

These three stages: Inspiration, Struggle, and Transcendence occurred on a grand scale in my journey to Torah observance, and that is why the book is organized into these three parts. However, this process repeats itself over and over again, albeit on a smaller scale, throughout our lives. That is because the work is never "done": to achieve our G-d-given potential is the journey of a lifetime. Indeed, after ten years of Jewish observance, many of the mitzvot have become so ingrained and part of my routine that I have to work to stay inspired. Nevertheless, I find that each

---

*   Akiva Tatz, *Living Inspired* (Jerusalem: Targum Press, 1993).

time I delve into Torah learning, I quickly become reenergized to keep growing in my connection with myself, others, and Hashem.

To live a Torah life in the Western world today is nothing short of a miracle; the society we live in constantly bombards us with the false message "that our existence is entirely superficial and sensual, that life is nothing more than a series of randomly unfolding events. Accordingly, our purpose is to grab hold of whatever temporary pleasure we can."[*] This attitude distances us from Hashem and a life of deeper meaning.

Not only do we face constant threats to our spiritual growth, but now we fear for our very lives, as anti-Semitic attacks increase at an alarming rate. Just prior to her death in 2016, Rebbetzin Esther Jungreis, *a"h* (an acronym for the Hebrew words meaning "may peace be upon her"), a Holocaust survivor and holy rebbetzin, wrote her last column entitled, "I'm Afraid." In it, she wrote, "I smell the noxious fumes of pre-Hitler Europe…" However, it was not the anti-Semites that she feared. Rather, she wrote, "What I *do* fear is our own people — yes, our own people who have forgotten who we are, who no longer remember that we Jews stood at Sinai, that we heard the voice of G-d, that we belong to a priestly kingdom, a holy nation, and that everything that befalls us is choreographed by Hashem and is a reflection of our own deeds, our own hands… We have shed our priestly garments and no longer recognize ourselves…"[**]

She continued, "Time and again G-d sends His prophets to remind us that our destiny is different from that of the other nations, that our very existence is directly linked to our adherence

[*]   Yossi Katz, *The Rebbe's Shabbos Table* (New York: Breslov Research Institute, 2019), 70–72.

[**] Rebbetzin Esther Jungreis, "I'm Afraid," *The Jewish Press*, August 19, 2016, https://www.jewishpress.com/judaism/ rebbetzins-viewpointrebbetzin-jungreis/im-afraid/2016/08/19/.

to G-d's commandments… And yet we fail to heed His messages, and that is what I fear… When will we wake up? When will we don our priestly garments and fulfill our G-d-given destiny and be 'a light unto all mankind'?"

The rebbetzin's words encapsulate why I wrote this book. The title, *Princess without a Crown*, refers to a lost Jew who is estranged from her regal heritage. To any Jew who does not have a real and deep connection to Hashem and His Torah.

It is my hope that in reading this book, you are inspired to reclaim your Jewish identity, whatever that means for you. We each have a special role to play in *am Yisrael* (the Jewish nation), otherwise we wouldn't be here. Although this book captures my unique journey, the story is universal in that Hashem is always with each of us, sending us messages through the people and events in our lives. I bless us that we should see Hashem's hand in our lives and respond to His messages for us. That we should connect with our G-d-given soul and express it in the world. That we should not be afraid to travel our own path.

I hope you enjoy reading about my journey.

With blessings,
Jenna Maio

Acknowledgments

THERE AREN'T ENOUGH WORDS TO express my gratitude to Hashem for the countless blessings He has given and continues to give me each and every moment. As our Sages teach, I opened for Him a hole the size of the eye of a needle, and He opened for me a world beyond my wildest imagination. He gave me the idea to write this book and the ability to write it. I am so grateful for my lot in life and His clear hand in it.

Thank you to my amazing parents, Paul and Jaime, for your unwavering support and encouragement. You are true *baalei chesed* (masters of loving-kindness and giving). I know it hasn't always been easy, but your belief in me gave me the confidence to become the person I am today. Thank you for letting me fly. All of my accomplishments and good deeds are yours. You should have long lives of health and *nachas*.

Thank you to my Grandma Bea for always believing in me.

Thank you to my brother, Mark, for your sense of humor and unwillingness to let this book collect dust on a shelf.

Thank you to Rabbi Baruch Yehuda Gradon, *shlit"a* (an acronym for the Hebrew words meaning "may he live a good, long life"), for always making time to answer my personal and professional questions. Your *daas Torah* (Torah wisdom) and sensitivity are unparalleled and I am both humbled and grateful to call you my *rav*.

Thank you to my rebbetzin, Ruthi Lynn. Your incredible clarity, strength, and *mesirus nefesh* (self-sacrifice) for *klal Yisrael* (the Jewish people) will forever inspire me. Thank you for guiding me through all of life's up and downs and laughing with me through everything.

I want to thank Rav Moshe Weinberger, *shlit"a*, of Aish Kodesh. Several years ago, I came to you with this book idea, and you encouraged me to write it. Thank you for showing me what it means to have a burning love of Hashem and Yiddishkeit (Judaism).

Thank you to my close friend and mentor Illana Moskowitz. You and Keith opened your hearts and home to me from the moment we met, and my life was never the same. You have taught me so much. Thank you for showing me how to "live aligned."

Thank you to my close teachers and mentors: Rabbi Shmuel Lynn, Rabbi Yehoshua Styne, Yehudis Golshevsky, Sara Yoheved Rigler, Jackie (Engel) Glaser, and Yael (Seruya) Zdanowitz. Your teachings, advice, and example give me strength and clarity to become a true *eved Hashem b'simchah* (servant of Hashem with joy).

Thank you to the Fleshels and Lipskiers of Emory University, who gave me my first taste of Shabbos and Yiddishkeit. Thank you to the Lynns, Spinkas, and Rudensteins at the University of Pennsylvania, who continued giving me many delicious tastes of Shabbos. Thank you for opening up your homes to countless students.

Thank you to Madelyn Kent for opening up the pathway to creative writing for me again through your incredible Sense Writing program.

Thank you to Linda Sivertsen, the "Book Mama," who gave me the confidence to finish writing this book. I came to you with an initial draft and notes and you saw the potential in this story. Thank you for believing in me.

Thank you to my creative mentor, Robert Avrech, for believing in me and encouraging my creativity.

Thank you to Kate Zentall, my first editor, who so efficiently cleaned up this text while maintaining my voice. It was a pleasure working with you.

Thank you to my first readers, Beth Tarica, Jaclyn Tarica, Jen Weber, Rebbetzin Sara Casen, Amanda Lynn, Nina Adler, Paige Wechsler, and Lani Harrison for your initial encouragement and feedback, which was invaluable.

Thank you to Rechy Frankfurter, editor of *Ami* magazine, for publishing this book as a serial column in *Ami Living*. I appreciate your openness and willingness to publish the book so that *frum* readers could get a real glimpse into the journey of a *baal teshuvah* (literally, "master of repentance"; someone who has chosen to live a Torah-observant life). Thank you also to Gitty Chein, who efficiently organized the publication of each chapter.

Thank you to Rabbi Eliyahu Miller of JewishSelfPublishing for helping me to publish this book with such enthusiasm. You truly made this process a joy and I am very grateful. Thank you also to Chaya Silverstone, my copy editor, for putting the final editorial touches on this book. And thank you to Shanie Cooper of Virtual Paintbrush for designing a beautiful cover with kindness and patience!

And finally, I want to express my deepest gratitude to my husband and best friend, Justin. You gave me the confidence to call myself a writer, you encouraged me to write this book, and you made sure I did it! This book simply would not have happened without you and your *mesirus nefesh*. Thank you for inspiring me to be my best self and supporting my dreams every day. You are a true life partner and I love you so much.

Part I

INSPIRATION

CHAPTER I

Princess without a Crown

April 2007

I WAKE UP IN A daze. The bed next to me is empty, covered in a mess of crumpled sheets and clothes. My hand shakes as I reach for water on the nightstand.

Through the space between the curtains, I catch a glimpse of my friends hanging out by the pool, laughing and basking in the good weather. I can faintly hear the music playing. I shiver and pull the covers closer to me. I feel awful in every possible way.

I'm in the Bahamas for my school's senior-year spring-break trip, a trip I begged — no, told my parents that I was going on. Yet this morning I wake up and I know that I am done. I am done trying to escape my own life.

For some reason, the only thing that can comfort me is to sing the lyrics of Matisyahu's "King Without a Crown" over and over again to myself in a quiet whisper:

> *If your cup's already full then it's bound to overflow*
> *If you're drowning in the waters and you can't stay afloat*
> *Ask Hashem for mercy and He'll throw you a rope*
> *You're looking for help from G-d you say He couldn't be found*
> *Looking up to the sky and searchin' beneath the ground*
> *Like a King without his Crown...*

Looking back, I wasn't singing to myself that morning in the Bahamas. I was calling out for help. The yearning was deep and subconscious, yet I can point to this very moment as the turning point where I felt, *I want to be good. I want a connection to something greater.* I didn't know how this was going to manifest itself, but that morning G-d threw me a rope and I grabbed it, and with His help, I started walking in the right direction. Little did I know how lost I had really been and how far I had yet to go.

CHAPTER 2

From One Bubble to Another

December 2007

I HAVE AGREED TO BE Randi's college roommate sight unseen. Our mutual best friend, Jaclyn — Randi's camp friend and my school friend — has fixed us up in a kind of arranged marriage even before Randi and I are both accepted at our first-choice school, Emory University. Such is the strength of Jewish Geography; everyone is connected in one way or another through friends from school or camp. And this common link is so strong that we trust it blindly.

Randi and I finally meet in person on a night out in New York City, just hours before we find out if we have gotten in. Standing on line outside a club, we hug each other and jump up and down, excited for the friendship that is to be, assuming we'll both get accepted.

Hours later, as I'm sliding into a cab, I get the email on my BlackBerry: I got in! I call Randi immediately; she did too.

What's a Jewish girl from New York doing going to school in Atlanta? I'm not so sure myself. My mom heard about Emory and encouraged me to visit. It's the most beautiful school I have ever seen and the most prestigious that my grades allow.

As most of my high school friends head off in groups to their respective schools at the Universities of Wisconsin-Madison, Michigan, and Maryland, I imagine I will be something of an exotic creature at Emory.

During the first few days of orientation, however, I realize this isn't to be the case. Emory, it turns out, is a hotspot for northeast Jewish kids. Before I have a chance to get settled, Randi and I are invited to parties and dinners that will hasten our reinitiation into the only social bubble we have ever known.

As we get ready to go out one night, Randi and I talk about which classes we'll take. I tell her I'm going to major in English and creative writing. Since I know I'll be going to law school afterward, I figure I can major in pretty much whatever I want.

My mother decided early on that I would go to law school and achieve the dream that had eluded her. She later admitted to me that when I was a child she would finish the stories she read to me not with "And they all lived happily ever after," but something to the effect of "And she went on to law school and was success-ful and financially independent and got married and lived hap-pily ever after." I have no recollection of this, but it may explain why law school has been something so ingrained that I've hardly questioned it.

Randi and I are picked up in an Audi by a few sophomore and junior girls Randi knows from camp. On our way to dinner in Buck-head, Atlanta's upscale neighborhood, we talk about rushing (the process of joining) sororities. At Emory, the social life for anyone who is anyone is Greek. The girls are in AEPhi, the Jewish sorori-ty. We aren't allowed to reveal that we've gone to dinner together, they tell us, since rush doesn't officially start until second semes-ter. But we don't have to worry, they say, because we will for sure be accepted into AEPhi too.

Just as it has been decided that I will be a lawyer, it has been de-cided that I will be part of this exclusive Jewish social group even before I step foot in the sorority house, because I come from the right hometown and I have the right friends and the right look. I wear black leggings, Uggs, and a sweatshirt, the unofficial JAP uniform, just like everyone else. Yet somewhere deep inside I wonder whether this is what I want. As comfortable as it feels to be in the only social world I've known, a part of me longs to break free and for once do my own thing. I just don't yet know how to make that happen.

In my first semester of college, I take the required English 101 course. My professor chooses to title our particular class "Repetition and Rebellion in the American Suburb." It is in this class that, for the first time, I begin to process the world I've come from.

I know repetition. I know the expectations of my social universe growing up: Conform, or be excluded. To be popular, one has to be good-looking or wealthy, with few exceptions. Those who are very good-looking and very wealthy are untouchable, and even if their personalities are dry or obnoxious, people still float around them.

I had enough of both to be accepted into this group from the start. Plus, I had two other assets: I was kind and my parents would drive us anywhere we wanted, whenever we wanted. Still, if I wanted to remain in the popular crowd, additional, unspoken rules had to be followed: I needed to wear stylish, upscale clothes. I needed to have an extravagant bat mitzvah party. I needed to get my nails done on a regular basis. I needed to go to the right parties. My parents needed to drive fancy cars. And I needed to get a car just as fancy as theirs when I turned seventeen.

The materialism of Long Island's Five Towns is embedded in its DNA. So are certain pilgrimages: trips to the gourmet cheese store during lunch break for custom-flavored iced coffee in Styrofoam cups; trips to the mall or the Miracle Mile on the North Shore for designer accessories on weekends; trips to the Atlantic Beach clubs and the Hamptons after a summer spent at sleepaway camp or on a luxury teen tour.

Along with this materialism comes an intense focus on body image, where only "scooped out" bagels and low-fat tuna are acceptable, and if you are ordering an omelet, it better be egg whites only with no butter or oil.

I once overheard a woman speaking to a middle-aged alumnus of my high school, expressing fear about working in the Bronx, since it is known for poverty and crime. The alumna answered, "You don't know fear until you walk down the halls of Hewlett High School in the wrong outfit." This was my normal, my repetition.

We conformed, my family and I, though it didn't come as naturally for us as it appeared to for my friends and their families. Even though my father was born and bred in the Five Towns, he was not a "lifer" at heart. He didn't care much about clothing. The har-ah! (In Long Island-ese: "The horror!") My father was not a high-powered businessman but a kindhearted musician. My mom's love of shopping compensated for my dad's deficiency in that area, but was hampered by the fact that we didn't have quite as much money as most of my friends' parents, who were loaded or at least appeared to be. Our attempt to keep up felt forced. For this reason and others I couldn't identify at the time, I felt like I never truly belonged.

Rebellion. Life in the suburbs became real boring real fast. My friends — good Jewish kids with too much money and time on their hands — coped by having parties and wasting their time on useless, hedonistic endeavors. Several ended up in rehab. On reflection, this form of rebellion of high school teenagers is so common it can be a repetition itself, deeply woven as it is into the fabric of secular American suburban life.

One thing that saved me, and one reason I never truly belonged, was my secret rebellion: *I liked school* — even though I would never admit it. Unlike many of my closest friends, I was in honors and AP classes. This separation was essential. They could never tell me, "Let's go out tonight, there's no homework." Weekends we'd hang out, but Sunday and weeknights were mine.

My honors classmates were part of the larger popular group, but were also fiercely competitive academically. Many of their parents, highly successful, put pressure on them to attend the best college possible. These students would fight with teachers for a few extra points on their assignments or exams, even if they got a ninety-five. Anyone who could claim a learning disability did so to nab extra time on the SAT. I was fortunate to have parents who encouraged but never pressured, and so I didn't have to resort to this behavior.

Once I was accepted to college early decision the fall of my senior year, I caught a bad case of senioritis: another repetitive rebellion in American suburbs.

One Saturday night during my senior year, a few friends and I ventured into the city to celebrate Elyse's birthday. Elyse epitomized what was untouchable: gorgeous, petite, and from a wealthy, beautiful family. We started the night with dinner at upscale Philippe, a restaurant Elyse was familiar with. Her older sister had preordered a bottle of champagne for us, and so we toasted her.

A bit later we noticed a table nearby of well-dressed guys who looked to be in their late twenties or early thirties. We started talking to them, taking care not to mention we were still in high school. Through my friends' older siblings and cousins, we knew some people in common. Soon they invited us to join them in the VIP room. Intrigued, we followed them to the back of the restaurant, behind a curtain and into an intimate space with a few small tables, couches, a TV, and music. Waiters produced more drinks.

We told them we planned to go to Marquee, a club where Elyse's cousin had reserved a table for us. They were headed there too, they told us; did we want a ride? Outside, a black Suburban truck awaited. At the club, the guys' table turned out to be next to ours. Free drinks, amazing music; we were in heaven.

Nights like these were the height of pleasure in my world. When I got home, usually just in time for curfew, I would quietly walk up the stairs and past my parents' bedroom, where I would hear the TV droning or else maybe a faint snore. I would toss my coat and bag onto my bed and stand alone in the dark for a moment. No matter how great the night was, I always somehow felt deflated.

A few months later, that morning during senior spring break in the Bahamas, I realized through my haze that I'd had enough. A passive player in my own life, I wanted to be actively present again. I arrived in Atlanta in the fall to start college both depleted and hungry for what else life had to offer.

CHAPTER 3

New Beginnings

It turns out someone else has arrived in Atlanta needing a new start: Professor Benjamin Reiss, who teaches my freshman seminar, American Literature and Human Transformation of the Environment. A Hurricane Katrina refugee, he'd been forced to flee his New Orleans home with his family just two years prior and plant roots elsewhere.

He is still processing the event, which is why he's teaching the seminar on how humans and the environment have affected each other over time. As we read Henry David Thoreau's *Walden* and Elizabeth Kolbert's *Field Notes from a Catastrophe*, I begin to think about not just my suburban hometown of "little boxes on the hillside," as Pete Seeger sang it, but the global world I live in.

This class resonates intensely for me, harkening back to an experience I had one day in my senior year of high school. Sitting on my bed after school and flicking through the TV channels, I came upon Al Gore's documentary on climate change, *An Inconvenient Truth*, and watched in horror as I learned we were threatening the earth's ability to sustain humanity. Panicked and helpless, I resolved to learn more about climate change when I got to college.

In Professor Reiss's class I absorb the environmental effects of the colonization of America, the Industrial Revolution, our twenty-first-century capitalist consumer culture, and the urgency of reversing — and certainly acknowledging — climate change. In

Anthropology 101 I learn that our culture is changing rapidly, even as human biological makeup has held pretty much steady since we first inhabited the earth.

All of this spells emergency to me. Things are spinning out of control. Walking through campus, I can't understand how no one else seems alarmed. "Hello!" I want to say. "Did you hear about climate change? That we're setting our planet on fire? That we're committing mass suicide as a species? *We have to do something!*"

Thankfully, I have friends to share my thoughts with. Many weeknights after we get enough work done, Randi and I go up to the roof with Zack and Drew, two guys who live on the floor above us. In the quiet fall night, we sit in a circle and talk about pretty much everything, starting off casually, reminiscing about our childhoods and high school or the latest popular TV episode, before segueing into something deeper.

"How crazy it is that our society has changed so much, so quickly since the Industrial Revolution, but that it's only a blip in human history?" I venture.

"Yeah," Zack jumps in. "We're all moving faster, but where are we moving *to*?"

"It's scary," I agree. "With climate change happening, we need a whole shift in the way we get our energy and the way we consume things. I just don't understand why more people don't care. We're the responsible ones; America is using most of the world's resources and energy, and eventually we'll run out."

"But Jenna," Randi reminds me, "it's hard for people to rally behind climate change because it's such an abstract issue. People aren't seeing it in front of their eyes."

I know she's right. "But we still have to do *something*," I say. "I feel like *I* have to, anyway."

"Have you seen Thomas Friedman's latest article?" Randi asks. We shake our heads. "He writes about how our generation is 'Generation Q'; we're too quiet given the massive issues of our time. Facebook 'likes' as our form of protest isn't going to cut it."

"Exactly!" I answer. I ask her to send me the article. I didn't know it was possible to have conversations like this with friends.

In the midst of my awakening, Randi asks me to come with her to her father's fiftieth- birthday party in New York City. No need to book a flight, she tells me; we're taking a private plane. She asks me not to tell anyone, though; she doesn't want to draw that kind of attention to herself. I'm impressed. Most of the people I grew up around only wanted that kind of attention.

That weekend, from the moment the black car shows up outside our dorm to take us to the airport, we are bathed in luxury: limos, suites in a five-star Manhattan hotel, ice-sculpted bars, celebrity appearances. Through it all, Randi is her same kind, down-to-earth self. I learn firsthand that it is possible to be both wealthy and humble.

And I realize that although I'm not nearly as rich as Randi's father, I'm still, like other upper-middle-class Americans, among the 1 percent richest people in the world. With this privilege I can do anything if I put my mind to it. I understand for the first time that my potential to affect change in the world is truly limitless. To me, this empowerment also carries with it tremendous responsibility.

I decide I will indeed go to law school, but I will learn the law in order to change it. I will find ways to stop climate change, to protect our planet and humanity.

Before I know it, I'm on a bus with students from the Emory Environmental Alliance headed for the state capitol building, where we will lobby Georgia senators to pass climate-change legislation. For the first time in my life, I feel that I'm standing up for something real.

Unfortunately, hardly any of the state congressmen who are supposed to eat lunch with us show, sending their secretaries instead.

While three of the secretaries enjoy their donated Whole Foods lunch, I pull up a chair. After they insist that they know what climate change is, I discuss the proposed state bills for a renewable energy portfolio and a ban on mountaintop coal as an energy source. The ladies nod politely as I speak and periodically offer a "wow" or "sounds good." I then ask, out of curiosity, whether they think climate change is real. The oldest one of the bunch, old enough to be my grandmother, looks up at me from her plastic plate and says, "I am a Christian, and I believe that our Maker put us on this earth and will take care of us as He always has." The other two nod in agreement.

I guess you'd rather await the building of the second Noah's ark, I think. Until then, I had never met anyone who had heard of climate change yet wholeheartedly denied its reality. I thought that such an awareness would lead to effective action. At that moment I understand that preventing the Flood will not be so simple.

Spring 2008

During the second semester of my freshman year, an opportunity falls in my lap, one that I was waiting for without knowing it.

A senior in the environmental club who spent the previous summer interning at a progressive think tank in Washington, DC, approaches me. The think tank funds student-run magazines on every major college campus in the country, but we don't have one at Emory. Would I like to start it? I could focus the magazine on anything I wanted.

Me? Start a magazine? I had written for my high school paper and recently began writing for the *Emory Wheel*, but I have no editorial experience. Founding a campus magazine seems overwhelming. But the prospect is also thrilling. Finally I can present and discuss issues of our time and encourage students to act. English businessman Richard Branson once said, "If someone offers you an amazing opportunity and you're not sure you can do it, say yes — then learn how to do it later." And that is exactly what I do. I decide to call the magazine *Generation Response*, a literal response to Thomas Friedman's "Generation Q" article.

With my focus on being part of the universal, global community, I resist being boxed in with the Jewish sorority, aligning myself with girls too often focused on shopping, partying, and getting their MRS degree. Of course they're not all like that, but there is a truth to the stereotype. Another sorority catches my attention. It isn't one of the "cool" ones, like AEPhi. The girls are not from my world. They are diverse and generally more grounded, though also nerdy and eccentric. I can't help noticing their motto, "To Be Rather than to Seem to Be." The irony does not escape me.

I'm sitting alone at my dorm room desk on a Sunday morning when an envelope slides under the door. It's bid day, when I find out which sorority I've been matched up with. I open the envelope: "AEPhi is proud to welcome you to the pledge class of 2008…" I toss the card on my bed and begin to cry. I'm frustrated at myself for not being strong enough to go my own way yet. That I've put myself right back in the same bubble I longed to escape throughout high school. I manage to conceal my puffy eyes before Randi comes back to the room. She's thrilled that I've decided to join AEPhi with her. I'm grateful for her and the other girls I know in our pledge class who have some depth. Maybe it won't be so bad.

At the weekly chapter meeting, after the issue of when our next mixer is and what the theme will be is hotly debated, I make my announcement about recruitment for *Generation Response*. I'm met with silence and a few polite smiles.

Despite my desire to deactivate my membership, which creeps up every now and then, I remain in AEPhi. Emory isn't such a big school, and I don't want to be the focus of people's gossip and stares. Besides, I actually do like some of the girls there. They understand me and the world I come from, which isn't something to take for granted. I appreciate this even more after noticing the socioeconomic and cultural gaps between me and my friends in the environmental club and in *Generation Response.* Yet I also realize that I can branch out. Even with my roots in the northeast Jewish AEPhi community, I can still be an environmentalist and a magazine editor.

CHAPTER 4

Shabbat Dinner with Matisyahu

THE FIRST TIME I GO to a Shabbat dinner on campus is in my sophomore year.

It has never occurred to me to go to Chabad or Hillel for Shabbat dinner. Only the really Jewish kids go to Shabbat dinner, like my classmates Rebecca and Brendon from freshman seminar. One day early in the semester, before the professor had come into class, I heard them talking about going home for Rosh Hashanah. *Going to New York for Rosh Hashanah?* I wondered. *We just got to school!* I couldn't believe that the holiday was so significant to them that it warranted a flight home.

Sure, I identify myself as a member of the tribe, because I happen to have been born Jewish. When people ask me my religion, my default response is, "Culturally Jewish, but spiritually other."

But this week I decide to go to Shabbat dinner because tonight is different from all other nights: Tonight, the Jewish reggae rap star Matisyahu is on tour in Atlanta and will be the special guest at the Emory Chabad.

Despite my excitement, I'm late for the meal. I approach the large tent behind the Chabad House, where the Chabad couple hosts anywhere from fifty to one hundred students each week. From inside, a warm light radiates. I can hear students talking and laughing. I catch the comforting aromas of chicken soup and challah. Just then, a religious man happens to walk out of the tent. This must be Matisyahu, I think, registering the black pants with tzitzit, the white strings hanging down from the corners of his undershirt. It's so meant to be! I can't believe it.

"Hi," he says. "Do you need a place to sit?"

Why does Matisyahu care if I need a place to sit? He looks around the packed tent for an open space. *Wow, he is so down-to-earth and nice!*

Above the chatter, I say, "It is such an honor to meet you. I am such a big fan."

"Thank you," he answers with a smile. When he shows me to my seat, someone else calls out to him, "Rabbi!" and I realize I have confused the Chabad rabbi with the rap singer. I am mortified. All of the bearded Orthodox men in black and white look the same to me!

I spot the real Matisyahu on the other side of the long table. After he speaks to the group and the meal is winding down, I find the courage to approach him. I have so many things I want to ask. What is it like to be Jewish, religious, and a rapper? Why did he become religious?

Instead I say, "Hi. I'm a big fan of your music. Thank you. I just wanted to ask, what do you think of the rapper Lil Wayne?"

I know. Of all things to ask. I could have told him that "King Without a Crown" saved my life. That it was the song in my soul when I didn't know I had a song left. But lately I just can't figure out why Lil Wayne is famous. The fact that he is scares me; it seems a sign of America's degrading culture. My friends are obsessed with him, but as far as I'm concerned, he is leading my generation astray into a realm of egotism, hedonism, and oblivion. A realm I've been edging away from since high school. His raps about meaningless things are indulgences the hour cannot afford. Maybe Matisyahu sees something I can't.

"I really have nothing to say about him," he answers. I guess he doesn't. I want to ask him more questions, like why he became religious, but I'm embarrassed at the seeming shallowness of my first question, so I go back to my seat with my tail between my legs.

CHAPTER 5

Birthright

Spring 2009

IT IS BEYOND ME (AND apparently Matisyahu) that I can't get my generation to care about mass extinction of the human race, but Lil Wayne has them in the palm of his hand.

I find solace in kindred spirits that had similar struggles in their time and place. In my Romanticism class, I meet William Wordsworth, who advocates for a return to nature before the Industrial Revolution wipes it out. In my Religion and Ecology class, I meet Ralph Waldo Emerson, a transcendentalist who connected with the Divine aspect of nature. In my World History class, I write about John Lennon, the song "Imagine," and his quest to elevate the consciousness of mankind.

As focused as I am on the outside world and its issues, these new friends of mine encourage me to turn inward. I am guided by my Religion and Ecology professor, who is a special woman. She believes in experiential education and so encourages us to begin each class with a meditation. This is how I learn to meditate. For homework, instead of work on the computer, we're asked to sit in nature, meditate, and record our reflections.

I begin to meditate, if not daily, at least weekly. Once my mind quiets, I can access a deeper part of myself, an inner voice that is often stifled by the fast-paced world trampling over it. It doesn't take much time for me to understand that there *is* something Divine in nature. This higher energy I sense is also within me; I can feel it sometimes when I meditate. I am not sure what to call it yet.

As I explore romanticism, transcendentalism, universalism, and Buddhism, my friends and I apply to go on a Birthright trip to Israel. In my mind, one has nothing to do with the other. Birthright is not an opportunity to learn about my own religion. It's a free vacation with friends, a chance to see Israel and meet a nice Jewish guy. It's just one of those things you "do." You go to college, you go on Birthright, you study abroad, you get a job in NYC, you get married, then you move to Westchester or Long Island.

All of my friends get on the Birthright trip except for me. *That's strange*, I think. Who gets rejected from Birthright? It's 2009, during the recession and the Bernie Madoff scandal. There are rumors that Birthright had a cut in funding. Still, it seems weird that I'm the only one of my friends who gets rejected. I decide not to do anything about it; I'll just apply again next year.

Shortly after, I'm at a party when I begin talking to an acquaintance, someone outside the AEPhi social bubble. She had just gone on a trip to Israel run by MEOR, a Jewish outreach organization on campus, that previous winter break. "You must apply for the summer trip," she tells me. "It was amazing! I'll introduce you to the rabbi."

The next thing I know, I'm sitting in the Student Union at a table when a man in a black *kippah*, a sweatshirt, and jeans sits down. I shift in my seat and look around; students with backpacks walk together in small clusters. I'm not used to being seen in public with a rabbi.

We introduce ourselves. "So," he begins, "tell me, are you committed to marrying Jewish?"

I am offended by the mere question. "No," I answer. "If I really connect to someone in a deep way, I'm not going to not marry him just because he's not Jewish," I explain, proud of my position.

We argue this point for a few minutes. I don't think the meeting is going so well, so the rabbi surprises me when he says, "Okay, you can come on the trip."

June 2009

Once in Israel, I discover that we have been scheduled every morning to study Torah before our touristy ventures in the afternoon. My AEPhi friends view it as the "catch," the obligation in return for the heavily subsidized trip to the Holy Land. But I'm actually intrigued to learn what Judaism has to offer in terms of spirituality. I've studied Buddhism and Transcendental Meditation; I might as well give my own religion a fair chance.

We walk up the long, steep driveway through the gate and into Neve's main building. Neve, I'm told, is a seminary. To me, a seminary sounds like a convent, a place where nuns go. It is in fact a yeshivah for girls, a place where women study Torah. This particular school is unique in that it is for women who did not grow up observant, but you wouldn't know it from how everyone is dressed. As we enter the air-conditioned lobby of the main building, with students and teachers going about their business, I notice the women wear maxi skirts and long-sleeved shirts, with others in knee-length skirts with tights (tights, in this Israeli summer heat!). Now I understand why we were told to wear skirts and sweaters out of respect. Rabbis in black suits, beards, and black hats meander through the stream of women. Despite the oppressive dress code, everyone seems content, at least on the surface. The energy is light and happy as students hold their books and laugh with each other.

I am alternately curious and intimidated by the foreignness of it all; it's their turf, after all, and I'm the visitor. At Neve Yerushalayim, for the first time, I am taking my "religious Jews" box off the shelf of my mind, dusting it off, opening it, and allowing myself to actually see what's inside. Depending on what I find, I may erase the current labels — "ignorant," "backward," "oppressive," "sexist," "Jew-centric" — and relabel it something else. Maybe.

CHAPTER 6

My Hebrew School Experience

FULL DISCLOSURE: I GOT KICKED out of Hebrew school.

From third grade until my bat mitzvah, every Tuesday and Thursday, my mom would ferry my friends and me in her old black BMW station wagon to Hebrew school at Temple Israel of Lawrence, the oldest and largest Reform temple in the Five Towns. My dad had had his bar mitzvah there in 1962. I recall a black-and-white photo of him and my grandpa, shaking hands on the lawn in front of the temple's grand brick entrance on Central Avenue.

In *real* school, I did well and the teachers liked me, despite my propensity to talk in class. By the time Hebrew school rolled around, however, I was restless. Jaclyn and I were partners in crime, and our goal was to learn as little as possible.

I knew I was Jewish, but I didn't understand how learning about Hebrew or the holidays had any relevance to my life. No one in my family was religious, not even my grandparents. We didn't speak Hebrew at home. We already observed the major holidays, Rosh Hashanah and Yom Kippur, days I got to miss school and run around the temple basement and play with my friends. Chanukah was the festival of presents. Purim was the day I got to go to the temple carnival and throw a pie at our principal, Mr. Fox,[*] who stood behind a cutout pretending to be the villain Haman. Passover

---

[*] Name has been changed to protect privacy.

24

was the spring holiday when I got to dress up in nice new clothing and eat chocolate lollipops and chocolate-covered matzah. What else did I need to know? As far as I was concerned, I just needed to get through Hebrew school so I could have my bat mitzvah, my "Jewish graduation party," like everyone else.

Bar and bat mitzvahs were lavish affairs. If you were invited to one, the service was obligatory if you wanted to attend the parties with dignity (though if it was just an acquaintance you were celebrating, you might be able to get out of it). For the Saturday night bashes, we went to country clubs or fancy hotels, where we dipped our hands into hot wax, took pictures, and got custom T-shirts made. At one party, my friends and I got a twenty-dollar bill from *Sopranos* star James Gandolfini, who was a guest and client of the bar mitzvah boy's father. Celebrity appearances weren't common at these affairs, but usually they were paid to come and not the ones paying.

One day, in seventh grade, I was taking breaks from doodling in my notebook to pass notes with Jaclyn. As I handed her my note, Mr. Fox opened the door and said, "Jenna. Write down what you just learned from the teacher and come to my office."

"Oooh," the class snickered. My face turned red. I looked at Jaclyn. Somehow I was always the one who got caught. I had remembered vaguely what was going on in class, so I wrote it down as best I could and left the classroom. I headed down the narrow hallway and turned left into the main office. I was told to sit until Mr. Fox was ready for me.

That day all I got was a lecture and a warning from Mr. Fox. He would be watching me.

Later that year I got my first cell phone. It was my prized possession, a chunky little Nokia. Even though it was against school rules, I brought it with me to Temple Israel. There, Jaclyn and I hatched a plan. I would go to the main office and pretend I needed to call my mom. Then I would dial my new cell phone number, causing the phone, which I had left in the classroom, to ring and disrupt the teacher. It was perfect.

We executed the scheme, and naturally the teacher got upset and confiscated my phone. Next thing I knew I was sitting around a table in one of the classrooms with Mr. Fox, Jaclyn, and both sets of parents.

"Whenever it's just Jaclyn in school, there is no problem," Mr. Fox said. "But when Jenna is there, there's always a problem." I put my head down into my arms and cried.

Mr. Fox asked us to leave the temple. With our bat mitzvahs only a few months away, we joined a Conservative temple down the street out of desperation.

I had never seen my parents so disappointed in me. They were so looking forward to continuing the family generation of having a bat mitzvah at Temple Israel. It was then that I learned that disappointing your parents is worse than making them angry.

I wrote a letter to Mr. Fox and asked my mom to mail it for me. She told me she would, but she never did. Instead she saved it. "I don't want to be Jewish anymore," I wrote.

At Neve I open my notebook and prepare to take notes. My sorority friends sit behind me, discussing their plans for the evening. As long as we're able to get up and make it to classes the next morning, we're allowed to go out at night. I play with my om necklace, symbolizing Eastern spirituality, a signal that I am on a spiritual path and not about to be brainwashed into anything. It's part of the protective wall I've placed around my soul: I am not like you and I don't want to be like you. I'm just here to…observe.

I notice a handwritten sign on the closet door: Hashem loves you. *What is Hashem?* I wonder.

Enter Rabbi Baruch Smith, a man with a long white beard and a black hat. "Okay, ladies, let's get started," he says in a friendly South African accent. He begins drawing on the board. The vertical axis, he tells us, is spirituality. The horizontal axis is physicality.

"The more you engage in the physical world," says Rabbi Smith, "by definition, you are moving away from spiritual access. The higher your level of spirituality, the less bound you are to the physical world." Hmm.

Rabbi Smith draws another picture, this time of the layers of our worlds. The outer rim is our physical bodies, moving inward through our conscious psyche, our emotions, our intellect, and finally our heart.

"The heart," he says, "is the place of inner wisdom." I copy the pictures down into my notebook.

"There are two ways to get to this inner wisdom. One approach, popular in Eastern spirituality" — I look up. He knows about Eastern spirituality? — "is to smash through the barriers, meaning to limit the physical world as much as possible to attain great inner clarity. The Jewish approach is to use the physical world to align with inner truth." We stare at him, trying to absorb what he is saying.

"Think about it. Why would Hashem create a world if the whole purpose was to escape from it? We need to elevate and sanctify the world…" I realize Hashem must be a name for G-d.

Rabbi Smith speaks about the different levels of our soul, our animal instincts, and our higher desires and how free will works. I lean forward, thirsty for every word. All I can think as my hand scribbles across the page to get everything down is, *What is happening?*

The next day Rabbi Smith teaches us about Shabbat. All I know is that you can't use electricity on Shabbat. Phones and computers are forbidden, as are cars. I always know it is Shabbat when I see droves of religious people walking home from temple on Saturday.

"Just like G-d created the world in six days and rests on the seventh day," Rabbi Smith says, and pauses, "we create during the week and then experience what we have created up until that point on Shabbat.

"The prohibitions on Shabbat are based on the work of building the Temple," he continues. "The laws revolve more around creation than work. For instance, you can carry a heavy couch, but you can't write."

I write quickly in order not to lose anything, but I realize it's hard to simultaneously absorb what Rabbi Smith is saying while doing this. Standing before us, he closes his eyes as if speaking from another realm. "So too," he continues, "after we die, we experience ourselves as we are up until our death. This is why our sages describe Shabbat as a taste of the World to Come. In this world, we experience our lives as we have created them up until Shabbat each week. Ideally, each week we build ourselves into better, more perfected beings and experience a higher self each week."

"Doesn't all of this Shabbat stuff matter only if you actually believe in G-d?" Kat asks. She's done it; she's dropped the G-d bomb. Even though the teachers encourage us to ask questions, this is the first juicy one. We all turn back to the rabbi.

"Of course it does," he answers with confidence. "To be a Torah-true Jew means to believe in G-d and the divinity of the Torah."

Torah-true Jew. That sounds a lot better than Orthodox. I don't like that word. It sounds so rigid and cold.

"But G-d's existence can never really be proven," Kat snaps back.

"You're right that G-d's existence cannot be proven absolutely, but there are several theories and proofs that can allow one to conclude that G-d's existence is a greater probability than it is not," Rabbi Smith explains.

"I would never base my whole life around a probability of G-d's existence," Kat retorts.

"Oh, but you base your life around probabilities all the time. Think about it — remind me your name?"

"Kat."

"Kat, think about it: Not a single pragmatic decision we make is ever based on absolute proof. When we get into a car, there is no absolute certainty that we will not be in an accident. When we marry someone, there is no absolute certainty that the marriage will work out."

"Right," Kat interjects. "But belief in G-d should be able to be proved empirically, through experience rather than mere logic."

"Ah-ha. This is very important to understand: G-d's existence cannot be proven empirically, only philosophically. G-d is an infinite being: omniscient, omnipotent, and omnipresent. We, on the other hand, are finite: limited to space and time. Our knowledge is inherently limited. A full grasp of the totality of reality and the spiritual realms is beyond us."

"So you're saying I just have to *believe*," Kat replies sarcastically, alluding to the blind — and often ignorant — faith that is common in places like the American Bible Belt.

"Not at all," Rabbi Smith answers. "As I said, even though G-d's existence cannot be proved empirically, it can be proved philosophically. Of course, there are possibilities to explain a universe without G-d, but there are several theories that in totality point to a greater probability of G-d's existence: first cause, design, moral relativism, ontology, empiricism. There is also the actual study of Torah itself and the inherent holiness and perfect wisdom in the biblical Hebrew language. Not to mention the miraculous survival of the Jewish people throughout history..."

Kat's silence and the stillness in the room betray the fact that none of us have really done our homework and are in no position to speak about the existence of G-d.

"All we can do is look at the evidence and weigh the probabilities,"

Rabbi Smith continues. "Now, obviously belief in G-d is a major thing, and so the probability in favor of G-d's existence should be great. We don't have time to go into this now, but soon Rabbi Kelemen will be speaking to your group. He wrote *Permission to Believe*, which goes through several theories I am alluding to. You must remember, ladies, that even if you come to the conclusion that G-d exists intellectually, your emotions may hold you back. You need to be honest with yourself."

I look at Kat. Was she being emotionally honest in asking her question? Am I being emotionally honest as I take in all this new information? What filters do I have?

I always believed in G-d growing up; I prayed to Him every night before I went to bed. I couldn't fall asleep without praying for my family and for myself, that we should be healthy and given whatever I felt we needed at that time. When I got to college, I called myself an agnostic because I didn't feel comfortable arguing for the existence of G-d without really looking into the matter as an adult. I believed in a higher universal power governing reality, and sometimes it was so clear I was riding the tide of that current — I would just "happen" to run into the exact person I needed to speak to about something I didn't even know we needed to speak about, things of that nature. Even now, I feel like I was carried to Israel effortlessly. I got on this trip so last minute, in such a serendipitous way. And all of a sudden a doorway to Jewish wisdom is opening; a door I would not have had access to had I been accepted by Birthright. Maybe this higher power is G-d's hand? I'm not sure yet.

CHAPTER 7

My First Shabbat

WE SPEND OUR FIRST SHABBAT in Ramat Beit Shemesh, a religious neighborhood outside of Jerusalem. I'm glad to be placed with the same host family as my new friend, Cynthia. As with most organized trips, our group has developed a camaraderie where we laugh on the bus to inside jokes and sing along to music. Beneath that unity, though, there's an unofficial split between those who are connecting to the trip spiritually and those who are here just to have a good time.

Cynthia, like me, is in the former group. At Neve, we usually take our breaks together outside on the balcony and talk about what we learned, about life. We share our career aspirations, our hopes and dreams, and we connect.

As in Jerusalem, the homes in Beit Shemesh are all made of Jerusalem stone. By this point I am used to seeing men and women in religious garb walking on the streets, but the sight still intimidates me. I feel like an intruder, like I don't belong here.

Our bus driver drops us off near our host's home and we find the door with the sign, The Levines.[*] Cynthia and I are greeted by Mrs. Levine, a middle-aged American woman. She wears a long black skirt and her hair is tucked into a beret.

She welcomes us in and introduces her two children who are

---

[*] Name has been changed to protect privacy.

home that Shabbat, fifteen-year-old Penina and twelve-year-old Yehuda. *What strange names,* I think. "The others are away for the summer," she explains.

"How many kids do you have?" I ask.

"Six, *baruch Hashem,*" she answers.

I figured. I know from home that religious people like to have a lot of kids. I often saw mothers in town with as many as four young kids in tow. Large families are so foreign to me, having grown up with only a younger brother. In my extended family, having more than three kids is unheard of.

"When did your family move to Israel?" Cynthia asks.

"About ten years ago, *baruch Hashem.*"

Since we landed in Israel, I've been hearing this term *baruch Hashem* constantly. I learn it means "bless G-d." I realize it is used in place of saying thank you. Or when people ask, "How are you?" instead of saying, "Good," many will respond, "*Baruch Hashem.*"

After serving us some drinks in the kitchen, Mrs. Levine shows us to the guest room in the basement. I'm relieved we don't have to sleep on the same floor as the family. The room is simply furnished, with two twin beds, a dresser, and a wooden desk with a computer.

"Please let me know if you need anything else," she says. "Make yourselves comfortable. We're going to light candles in about an hour. There are towels in the bathroom if you want to shower before Shabbos."

"Thank you so much," Cynthia answers for both of us.

Cynthia and I are already dressed for Shabbat. I smooth out my light-colored printed skirt from Urban Outfitters. Cynthia is wearing a black maxi dress with a cardigan. We look similar, with our tall, slim frames and pale skin and brown hair. Her hair is straighter than mine, though, with only a slight wave to it. After all the years of beating my hair into submission with treatments, it's still curlier than I would like.

We take turns going online and checking our email and Facebook before Shabbat starts. We call our parents. Cynthia speaks to her mother in fluent Portuguese. She's originally from Brazil but grew up in Boca Raton, Florida, a northeast Jewish bubble of its own. I've been spending winter vacation in Boca since I can remember, because my grandparents, like those of so many others, live down there.

After Cynthia hangs up, she asks me if I'm turning off my phone for Shabbat. I tell her I'm going to try. After some discussion, we agree that we want to try to experience a real Shabbat, to "try on" some of the teachings we've been exposed to. I certainly feel I'm playing a part in a Jewish Bible play in my long skirt and cardigan.

When we go upstairs, I smell fresh challah baking and begin to salivate. Mr. Levine comes down the stairs and into the kitchen and we exchange hellos. He is dressed in a black suit and white shirt and is wearing a black velvet *kippah*. One of my MEOR counselors explained to me that different head coverings symbolize specific religious and political leanings. A white-knitted *kippah* represents a more Zionist outlook, whereas a black velvet *kippah* represents an emphasis on Torah over the State of Israel. All the rabbis on our trip wear black velvet *kippahs*.

Mr. Levine and his wife discuss the lighting. I know that all lights must be left on or off prior to Shabbat — they cannot be switched on or off once Shabbat starts. As they talk, Mrs. Levine puts food on a hot plate, which will keep the food warm for dinner tonight and lunch tomorrow.

"Good Shabbos," Mr. Levine says, before leaving to go to temple with his son. I recently learned that men are obligated to go to temple and pray in a minyan with a minimum of ten men, but women are not.

The dining room has a glass wall overlooking the vast mountains beyond the community of Beit Shemesh, and the view makes the modest-sized room seem endless. The mountains are naked, brown, and parched. The burning sun is beginning to fade, slowly drifting into the abyss for the night. Inside, Mrs. Levine and her Penina stand side by side before the tapered candles that sit in their silver candlesticks atop the dining room table. Mrs. Levine lights the candles with care, and then she and Penina quietly say the prayer, in Hebrew, of course.

I recognize the prayer, but am unable to understand it and so observe silently, like a spectator. I fret inwardly about whether we will have to go to temple. I've never been to an Orthodox temple before, not to mention one in Israel. After the prayer, Mrs. Levine turns to us and says, "Good Shabbos."

"Good Shabbos," we reply simultaneously. The words feel weird as they leave my mouth. I don't think I ever said them before.

"We're going to shul," she informs us. I guess we're going to temple after all.

We approach a small one-story building that stands alone on a patch of grass. *This is the temple?* I think. I thought Orthodox people take prayer seriously; why is the building so bare? There are two doors, one for men and one for women. We enter the one on the right. Women and girls are sitting at long tables in fold-up chairs. They sing along quietly with the men, who are on the other side of a wooden partition. The singing is a pleasant surprise; I had expected a strict, dry reading of prayers.

The chairs are all taken, so we stand in the back with several other women. Mrs. Levine hands me a prayer book, but I don't bother to follow along. My Hebrew isn't good enough. Besides, everyone here knows these songs as if they were written on their hearts.

The songs are stunning. Some women are swaying, others are rocking, and some cover their eyes with their hands. I stare into the thick ivory fabric at the top of the wooden partition to catch a glimpse of what's happening over on the men's side. I can make out that they are joyously singing and dancing in a circle.

As the rhythm and energy of the songs rise, it seems like each person's love, fears, hopes, and dreams are swirling together into a greater, combined energy. I imagine that each person's spirit is a flame, and through the song, all the flames merge into a larger flame, flaring up, reaching for something higher.

As we leave the temple, I feel ashamed for having judged it by its appearance. The service has been more heartfelt than anything I ever experienced in my temple at home, with its high ceilings, stained-glass windows, and intricate wood carvings.

We meet the men at home, where we are joined with another family, the Kirschners.* Mr. Levine and Mr. Kirschner are dressed almost identically. Mrs. Kirschner wears a colorful scarf to cover her hair, while Mrs. Levine wears what I think is a wig.

We take our places around the table and everyone begins to sing Hebrew songs that I have never heard before. Then Mr. Levine, who sits at the head of the table, places his hands on the heads of each of his children and whispers a blessing. He says the blessing over the wine for Kiddush, which is the one thing I'm familiar with.

"Now we wash our hands before we make *hamotzi*," he says to us, referring to the blessing on the challah. "Once we wash, we don't speak until we eat a piece of bread."

Mrs. Levine shows Cynthia and me how to wash our hands with a washing cup: two times on the right and two times on the left. Then we repeat a blessing after her. The beginning is the same as the other blessings, but I've never heard the ending before. I try to pretend that I don't feel like a complete idiot.

We sit down at the table and wait for everyone to finish washing hands. I'm impressed by the ability of a group of Jews to remain

---

* Name has been changed to protect privacy.

this quiet for an extended period of time; I never witnessed such a thing before. Mr. Levine makes the blessing on the bread and slowly slices it up. I stare at him, anxious for my piece. Time slows down. All we can hear is the knife cutting through the challah and onto the cutting board. Each person speaks only once he has eaten a piece of challah, to remark on how tasty it is.

After a few quiet moments, Mrs. Levine turns to me. "So, Jenna, where are you from?" Everyone starts taking salad, dips, and fish arrayed on the table.

"I'm from the Five Towns," I say, knowing they will recognize this area since it comprises a large religious community.

"Oh, the Five Towns," they say, delighted. "Which town?"

"Hewlett."

"Hewlett?" they say, puzzled. "We never heard of that one."

"That's the one no one ever knows about — that and Inwood," Mr. Kirschner interjects. It's nice to know I'm from the town that everyone forgets about. In my world, my secular Jewish friends only know of Hewlett; they don't know of Lawrence, Woodmere, or Cedarhurst, because no one they're friends with lives there. In my world, Hewlett is the main town, not the forgotten one. But I don't say that.

"Which high school did you go to?" my host asks.

"Hewlett High School," I answer, somewhat embarrassed, because I didn't attend one of the many religious schools in the area.

"What are you studying?" Mrs. Levine asks me.

"English and creative writing and environmental studies," I answer.

"Do you know what you'd like to do after you graduate?"

"I want to go to law school and work on climate-change policy issues." After the words leave my mouth, I wonder if they even know what climate change is.

Just then, Mr. Kirschner looks up from his plate and enlightens me. "Climate change," he says with a wave of his fork. "What a bunch of baloney." He looks back down and resumes eating. No one says a word.

I feel my face turn red. What does he know about climate change? I can't believe he can dismiss it so quickly without knowing what he's talking about. And to say it with such confidence? After I revealed that this is what I want to spend my life's energy on?

I don't understand: If Orthodox Jews believe that G-d created the world, how is it that I have found more sensitivity about G-d's world from non-Jews and Buddhists, in the writings of environmentalists Wendell Berry and Gary Snyder? Tears well up in my eyes.

I remain in the safe space of my own head for a while, being interrupted only to pass the salad. Finally, I realize something: Haven't I done the same thing my whole life with religious Jews and Torah? Dismissed them without really knowing what I was talking about? I feel like G-d is sending me a sign: *This is what ignorance is, Jenna. Don't fall into it, especially not with my Torah.* I calm down a bit and rejoin the conversation.

(In hindsight, I believe Mr. Kirschner's comment was incorrect; the Torah view doesn't necessarily disregard climate change. His insensitive statement and behavior are in no way representative of the Orthodox community. Most religious Jews I encounter are among the most refined people I know.)

CHAPTER 8

The Eternal Question

I sit on a couch in a corner of the lobby of the Novotel Hotel in Jerusalem and shift uncomfortably. Facing me is Rabbi Yehoshua Styne, a MEOR rabbi who also teaches at Machon Shlomo, a yeshivah for men who did not grow up religious. I signed up to meet with him because he comes from the same world I do, although you would never know it by looking at him now. I was surprised to learn that Rabbi Styne also grew up on Long Island in an affluent secular Jewish community. I'm hoping he can help me process the overwhelming amount I have learned and experienced in my three weeks in Israel. Amid the blur of people walking past us, sitting at the bar, and checking into the hotel, he asks me a question.

"Jenna, do you believe in G-d?" he asks.

"I think so," I answer. I recall all the times I prayed before going to sleep growing up. Where did that come from, I ask myself, if not from believing?

"Jenna. I don't *believe* in G-d; I *know* there is a G-d. I *know*."

How can someone know *there is a G-d?* I wonder. How did this man come to be so strong in his belief? He wasn't born into it, growing up nonreligious in Great Neck, New York. So...how?

After our meeting, I walk through the lobby feeling a mix of both great clarity and massive confusion. I have clarity that my spiritual journey is progressing, and I know what I need to do now: I need to get clear on whether I believe there is a G-d. If I decide that I do, and if I believe He gave the Torah to the Jewish people... *Am I going to be Orthodox?* There it is, the thought that I've dreaded. I feel sick, in a swirl of confusion. I don't even know what it means to be Orthodox! I'm not ready for this kind of change. I don't want it. But the thought is there.

CHAPTER 9

Back to Planet Earth

Summer 2009

I MANAGE TO SNAG A seat on the subway during morning rush hour. As we charge through the tunnels beneath New York City streets, I look around for a spark in someone's eye, but encounter only blank stares. Commuters are engrossed in their phones or the newspaper, lifeless, until the subway lurches to a stop. Then the doors open and the riders exit and enter in floods, hurrying, always hurrying.

The Jerusalem-stone building at Neve where I studied for three weeks seems a distant dream now, as the subway screeches on the tracks and I stare into its dark windows. Back from Israel, I feel disoriented, spit out from an alternate universe.

This summer marks my initiation into the rat race. I'm an intern in Senator Chuck Schumer's Manhattan office. In the morning I hurry to the Long Island Rail Road and then race to make the subway, so I can race to my office so I can sit at my computer screen for eight hours. After which I race back down into the subway so I can race to make the earliest train back to my parents' home on Long Island, where I'm staying for the summer.

I stare at an ad on the subway car: Life is too short to have a job you hate. Ironic, considering the subway is taking most people to the job they hate. *But life is also too short to live mindlessly,* I add to myself. I think back to my meeting with Rabbi Styne at the Novotel Hotel near the end of my Israel trip. I had been in a panic then. A disturbing thought had been eating at me in the days before our meeting: If I do believe that G-d exists and the Torah is true, doesn't that mean I must become Orthodox? I had buried the thought as quickly as it arose. But my meeting with Rabbi Styne brought it back, front and center, and shook me to my core.

Only my MEOR counselor, Jackie, could placate me. "You don't need to put this kind of pressure on yourself," she told me in her Australian accent. "Just keep learning when you go back to school, and you'll see what happens." I agreed. I would keep learning Torah, slowly, and eventually decide how "Jewish" I wanted to be.

As I sit in the intern area of Senator Schumer's office and process visa applications into the computer, I observe with a new interest the two Orthodox girls in our group. They wear skirts every day. At lunch, when we go out as a group, they come along with their homemade kosher sandwiches.

Where in Israel talk about G-d and reality was plentiful, here it is a rare commodity. I'm in the greatest concrete jungle on earth, filled with any material thing I could want, yet I feel I'm in a parched desert, thirsting for spirituality. Week after week at lunch I wait for the girls to speak words of Torah, like the teachers at Neve. It doesn't happen. I realize they are not necessarily interested in the spirituality of Torah; being observant is just who they are. For them it isn't a question whether they will wear skirts or eat kosher. For me it's a big question, followed by an exclamation mark.

Every Monday after work, I schlep to the Upper West Side to study Torah at Aish. Amid the sounds of honking horns and bus engines, I'm plagued with both determination and doubt. One voice tells me, *Jenna — what are you doing this for? You're crazy! Just go home like every other normal person. You're tired!* And it's true, I am tired. I want to go home. I can't, though. There was a light, a truth I had experienced in Israel, and I need to follow that light;

I need to follow it *now*. I can't just let it go and slip back into the dark abyss, where I may not be able to find it again back on campus in the fall. I already feel it slipping away.

One Monday, I walk toward Aish, hoping that I don't run into anyone I know. I haven't told my family and friends much about the trip to Israel or my new spiritual direction. They probably wouldn't understand, and I'm not in a place to defend it should I need to — and I will need to. After all, religion is the opiate of the masses, right? For ignorant, Bible Beltloving, backward-thinking people, right? And then, of course, I see my aunt and uncle walking toward me.

My aunt Lynn and uncle Jeff split their time between the Upper West Side, the Catskill Mountains in upstate New York, and their winter home in Arizona. Jeff's grandfather founded the Nevele Grand Hotel in the Catskills in the early 1900s, and it became the third-largest hotel in the area. In its heyday, Jews from all over the tristate area summered at the resorts that made up the "Borscht Belt." When my father was a child, his family spent time up at the Catskills, and that's where Aunt Lynn, my father's sister, met Jeff. In her teenage years, my aunt longed to escape suburbia. When she married Jeff in 1966 at age twenty-three, she left the Five Towns and never looked back.

My aunt wears an elegant, loose-fitting pantsuit that surely costs more than what I will earn this entire summer in Senator Schumer's office. She made her chunky pearled necklace in jewelry class, jewelry making being one of her hobbies, as is graphology, which she learned from my great-grandmother Essie. My uncle Jeff wears a sweater vest and holds two leashes tethering their two little pugs, Sange and Leopold.

"Hi, guys!" *Please don't ask me where I'm going.*

"Hi, Jen." My aunt kisses me on the cheek. "What are you doing here?"

Don't say where you are going. "I'm going to a Jewish class at Aish, this learning center a few blocks away." *Ugh, why do I always spill information when I'm put on the spot?*

They look at me, puzzled at the prospect of such a pursuit. Fortunately, they don't ask me to explain. I'm relieved when after some more small talk we part ways. I just hope my aunt doesn't tell Grandpa what I'm up to. Grandpa, the Reform Jew that he is, might be unsettled, if not horrified, that I'm investigating Orthodox Judaism.

Aside from these weekly jaunts to the Upper West Side, life continues for me pretty much as it was before my trip. One night my friends and I go to see Matisyahu perform in Central Park. Somehow, we get backstage. Matisyahu is in his trailer, just a few feet away. I want to go in there and ask him about G-d and life and becoming religious. I want to tell him how one of his songs changed my life.

But I hesitate. I've already made a fool of myself with Matisyahu once before. I decide not to bother him because he hasn't gone on yet and might be prepping. Instead, we go over to the stairs leading onto the stage and look out on the crowd of thousands, a pretty awesome sight. Some rapper is onstage warming up for Matisyahu. Another guy is standing with us on the stairs. We get to talking and it turns out he's another Jewish religious rapper, Kosha Dillz. I can't believe it! Just a few weeks ago in Israel, a friend on the trip told me about Kosha Dillz for the first time, and now, here he is, in the flesh!

When he joins the other rapper onstage and we watch them perform, I feel that G-d has somehow orchestrated this. Standing offstage, looking out over the crowd on that summer night in

Central Park, I feel G-d is telling me, "Jenna, I can take you back-stage, I can introduce you to celebrities, I can do anything. What are you going to do with it all?"

In the spaces between those inspirational moments, I read. I start with *Letters to a Buddhist Jew*, by Rabbi Dr. Akiva Tatz and Rabbi Dovid Gottlieb, which my counselor Jackie recommended. As I read it, I realize that everything that has resonated with me in Buddhism — meditation, prayer, a proper relationship with the physical world — is also right there in Judaism. Who knew? No wonder so many Jews are drawn to Buddhism.

I send an email to Rabbi Styne and update him on my progress:

> *Shalom, Rabbi Styne,*
>
> *I miss Israel so much! I definitely still have some of the energy from the trip with me, but it's hard going from Israel to Long Island, as you know. I was on an amazing spiritual high, which I find slowly withering away... I've been doing a little something each day to keep me close to Judaism and G-d. For example, yesterday I got Shabbat candles and the scroll for the mezuzah that I will put on my door when I get back to school. I just ordered some good books, one called Letters to a Buddhist Jew. As of now, I know G-d is here. The thing I need to be certain of is that He wrote the Torah. I'm hoping Torah study will help me...*

CHAPTER 10

Planting Seeds

Fall 2009

IN MY JUNIOR YEAR, I decide to live in the Seed House, an intentional living community focused on sustainability. The Seed House is nestled among trees in a cozy corner at the end of a tucked-away street on the far corner of campus. It is the last sign of civilization before the small patch of woodland that separates Emory's campus from the streets of Decatur, Georgia.

Our house is part of a pilot experiment, with us the pioneers, in trying out eco-friendly ways of living. To date we have gotten as far as unplugging electronics when we aren't using them, making a compost garden, and collecting shower water in a bucket to recycle in the toilets. I'm not so excited about that last one.

I check the time; I'll have to get ready soon. For the second week in a row, I'm going to the rabbi's for Shabbat dinner. I've asked Randi to come with me, but she didn't go on the Israel trip and doesn't seem too interested. As I shower and get dressed, I realize that my choice to connect to Judaism is separating me from my friends. Yet it also makes me feel special. I like that every week I have a retreat of sorts, a place where I can enjoy a home-cooked meal with other like-minded people. It feels homier to me than my Seed House community.

Rabbi Yaakov Fleshel lives in the religious community close to campus. As I ascend several flights of stairs, the voices of other guests gathered there grow louder. I feel nervous; I'm new to this scene. When I finally reach the apartment, I find about fifteen students schmoozing before the meal begins. I see a few familiar faces from the trip, but the rest are pretty much new to me. It's evident that most are regulars at the rabbi's, many having grown up observing Shabbat in some form. Just the fact that they make time for Shabbat each week easily makes them the most religious Jewish students on campus. I cling to my perception that this is a nerdier crowd than the one I'm used to, yet they, like me, look forward to Shabbat dinner as an oasis from the workweek. As we sit on the folding chairs at the long dining table, I begin to truly savor Shabbat — engaging in deep conversation, making jokes, and singing over wine, warm challah, and chicken soup. Time stands still, especially when I can't check my phone.

Next to me is a sophomore named David. We talk about our majors and our goals after graduation. He tells me, "I'm going to Harvard Law School." I laugh, but he's serious. He's a philosophy major, and before we know it the conversation turns to philosophy and religion.

As we start on dessert, one of the girls approaches the rebbetzin, and above the conversations I hear her say to our hostess, "I feel guilty because I'm going to a party after this." I too am debating whether to go out after dinner.

"Just say the bedtime Shema before you go to sleep at night," the rebbetzin tells her. I can't believe it. The rebbetzin doesn't make her feel guilty; she simply suggests a small act that will reconnect the girl to G-d. I begin to learn that growing Jewishly does not mean doing it all at once. It's okay to take it slow.

The semester takes on a rhythm. In between Shabbat dinner, classes, homework, working on *Generation Response,* going to the gym, and spending time with friends, I arrange to meet with Rabbi Fleshel once a week to continue learning Torah. But it's a challenge. I do want to learn Torah, but that flash of inspiration from the trip is dimming, overshadowed by, well, how *busy* I am. The irony is not lost on me: I can spend hours on minor exercises for professional advancement or waste blocks of time scrolling through my newsfeed to read about other people's lives, but when it comes to discussing the purpose and meaning of my life...I have to make a real effort to carve out a simple hour a week.

So when the rabbi tells me that Rabbi Yaakov Marcus, one of my teachers from Neve, is visiting to teach some classes and meet with students, I sign up for an appointment and then beat myself up about giving away a piece of my precious time. On the day of our meeting, I walk down the hall of the Student Union for our appointment. The old-style fifties building reminds me of young men in letter sweaters — surely no images of determined Jewish women like me; we've not come on the scene yet. Then my mind returns to the familiar world of my planner and begins to race through how I'm going to get everything done that day. *I guess I can do my outline for the English paper tonight, then gym and dinner — or maybe I should work on the magazine edits first?*

My head is still buzzing when I sit down at the table in the small conference room across from Rabbi Marcus, with his short white hair and clear brown eyes. He asks me if I have plans to return to Neve. I tell him I do not. I explain that this winter break I'm going with my family to visit my grandparents in Florida, like a good northeast Jewish girl. And then in the summer I hope to intern with an environmental lawyer, which is crucial for my law school applications. Rabbi Marcus asks me to consider coming back to Neve after graduation for the summer before law school.

"If you can stay connected enough to Jewish life here on campus to make it back to Neve after you graduate, you'll be able to build a strong Jewish and spiritual foundation for your life. You won't need to seek fulfillment from your career," he explains.

I don't want to admit that he's right, but he is: I am indeed seeking my primary fulfillment in life from my career. I'm so uptight about my schedule because I want to get into a top law school so that I can save the world through creating climate-change policy. This has been my primary motivation and source of meaning for the past three years. That, and the fact that my mom is counting on me to realize her own professional dream.

For the first time since I can remember, I create a personal goal: I resolve to return to Neve for their six-week beginner program after I graduate. For the next year and a half, then, I just need to stay connected to the light I saw, enough so that it can guide me back to where I found it.

CHAPTER 11
The Weight of Expectation

December 2009

WE DRIVE ALONG CLINT MOORE. Only a few luxury cars are on the wide, open road. People drive at a relaxed pace. This is Boca, after all. Also known as "G-d's waiting room," since so many people come down here to escape the New York rush for a more measured retirement and the following Great Beyond. We pass rows of palm trees lining the outer walls of the gated communities.

We pull up to the security gate of St. Andrews, among the ritziest of the Boca clubs, with its grand waterfall entrance adorned in festive lights.

"Remember," my mom says, turning back to look at my brother and me, "if Grandpa asks what we did today, just tell him we sat by the pool." (We went to the mall.) "And remember, Jenna," she says. "Don't bring up your new car."

I'll remember.

My grandpa, one of four children to Polish immigrant parents, grew up in a poor family during the Great Depression. He likes to tell the story of the time his family had to jump out of the window of their Brooklyn apartment because the landlord was at the door demanding the rent. When he met my grandmother, who lived on Park Avenue with her assimilated Jewish-American parents, he saw an opportunity for a better life. After he married Grandma, he joined her father's successful garment-center business in

Manhattan. My grandparents were among the first families to move out to the Five Towns in 1950 and soon after joined one of the local country clubs. There, Grandpa became friends with a Jewish Manhattan real estate mogul and eventually made several successful deals with him. Still, he never lost his Depression mentality. My grandma, despite being wealthy in her own right, was kept on a tight financial leash. She passed away when I was in high school. I remember, as a child, when we would go to the drugstore, she would almost always tell me to put back whatever trinket I asked her to buy because it was "too expensive."

The valet opens our doors, and as soon as I walk into the lobby of the club, I spot Grandpa, slumped in a tall leather armchair. He is early, as usual, making us late as usual.

"Hi, Grandpa," I say, smiling, and bend down to give him a little kiss on his bony cheek veiled with thin, wrinkled skin.

"Hi, darling," he says, smiling. He gets up and begins walking quickly into the dining room with his cane. He is too proud to admit that he needs a wheelchair. At ninety-three, he is obviously struggling. We follow him through the cocktail bar and lounge and head into the dining room.

As the hostess leads us to our seats, we pass by the lavish buffet. The meat station, the salad station, the kids' table, the dessert table. Waiters dressed in black suits hurry past us. Families stroll by, dressed in their finest resort wear, laughing.

After we are seated and the hostess smiles and turns to go back to her station, I feel a sense of shame. As I've gotten older, country clubs have made me feel uncomfortable. I don't think we are any better just because we're the ones being seated. At the same time, I'm grateful to be on this side of the table.

After we've had our salads and returned from the buffet with our dinner, my mom attempts to convince my grandpa that my brother and I are worthy. She starts with me, as usual. Leaning over, she strains her voice above the chatter in the club. "Henry, Jenna made dean's list again this semester."

He nods in approval.

"She got A's in all of her classes," she continues.

I wish he would smile and say something encouraging. To him, hard work is a given.

"So," he starts, looking at me, and then pauses for a moment. I sit on the edge of my seat. "What are your plans for after you graduate?"

My mom looks at me. Her eyes tell me, *Say the right thing or else.*

"I want to go to law school," I answer proudly.

"What type of law would you like to practice?"

"Environmental law."

"Environmental law doesn't make a lot of money." I expect this response and have an answer prepared.

"It depends who you work for," I begin, pausing to allow the waiter to top off our hardly touched water glasses. "If you work for companies and help them navigate environmental laws, you can make a good living." No need to tell him that I actually want to go into public policy.

He nods again. "And which law schools are you applying to?"

"Schools that have strong environmental law programs," I answer. "Berkeley, Pace Law School, Vermont Law School…" I can say anything at this point, since Grandpa never went to college and doesn't know from school rankings.

I watch him as he digests both his dinner and my words and considers his next question. His small, beady eyes focus down at his plate. His neatly trimmed nails, coated with clear polish, are poised on his fork and knife. I feel my heart beating in my chest.

"So tell me," he begins, as he slices into his rare steak. I relax, thinking perhaps he will move on from my professional aspirations. "How is your social life?" My grandpa cares about my social life because he wants me to make relationships with wealthy people, like he did.

"Good," I answer. "You know, my friends and I go to parties, or occasionally out to lunch or…dinner," I answer. He nods again. *Do not mention Shabbat dinner*, I remind myself. I almost slipped.

"What about you, Mark?" he asks, turning to my younger brother, who is still in high school. The spotlight is off me for tonight.

"I'll be right back," I say, getting up to go to the ladies' room. I make my way through the maze of tables and waiters, past the violinist playing classical music in the corner. Once I'm in the warm and empty restroom, I let out a sigh. I will stay here as long as possible, occupying myself with the array of soaps, lotions, and fresh towels until I must return.

CHAPTER 12

The Party That Changed My Life

Fall 2010

I LEARN WITH RABBI FLESHEL that while Judaism does say that man has free will to make moral decisions, there is a coexisting idea called *hashgachah pratis,* or Divine Providence. G-d's hand, so to speak, guides us at every moment of our lives. Nothing is coincidence. Everything is meant to be.

As someone who checks her horoscope daily and looks for signs obsessively, this concept comes naturally. I always felt I was being guided by a higher energy. Slowly, since the Israel trip, I have been calling that higher energy G-d.

It is October of my senior year, and my sorority has planned a date party. I hate these parties. Whenever I go just to make an appearance, I wander through the crowd like a vagabond, in search of someone to have a real conversation with. Usually these hunts are in vain, and I leave feeling more alone than I would have had I just stayed home with my books.

For some reason, though, I feel more than usually obligated to go to this one. At the party, I'm surprised to run into my friend David from Rabbi Fleshel's Shabbat table, the one who's intent on going to Harvard Law. (Which of course is exactly what eventually happens.)

I am relieved; I know David and I can at least have a good conversation. We find a table outside and talk. I tell him more about

my desire to do climate-change policy work. I tell him I'm applying only to top-ranked environmental-law programs, regardless of
their overall rankings.

This past summer my parents and I visited Bard College in upstate New York, which offers a master's in environmental policy
in a four-year joint degree program with Pace Law School. While
neither school is ranked particularly high generally, their environmental program seems truly innovative. I'm seriously considering
it, despite the prospect of living in the middle of nowhere at Bard
for at least a year.

"You cannot go to Bard," Rabbi Fleshel told me when I got back
to Emory. "It will kill you Jewishly." I know he could be right, but
I'm not about to forgo the perfect program. They have a Hillel on
campus, I tell myself. Despite my determination to return to Neve
and my continued studies with the rabbi and Shabbat dinners, my
professional goals still take precedence.

Speaking above the party music, I tell David what attracts me
to the program at Bard: the study of different environmental issues from science, policy, and economics perspectives. To know
the law alone is not enough, I tell him. To make effective climate
policy, I need to understand the issues from all sides.

"If you're really interested in interdisciplinary work," David says,
"you have to check out University of Pennsylvania Law School. It's
the best interdisciplinary law school in the country."

I don't think I'm Ivy League material. Still, as soon as I get home
I look up Penn Law and see that he's right; the school really does
facilitate joint degrees. I could get a law degree and a master's in
environmental studies in three years!

I realize I have to apply. But I can't get into Penn, I think. My
application is borderline at best. I know my only chance is to apply
early decision. Penn Law is one of the few schools I'm considering that even offer such an option. The application is due in about

a month. I take a deep breath and decide to go for it. What do I have to lose?

On December 8, 2010, about a month after submitting my application and two weeks before I'm scheduled to hear back from Penn, I'm in a store picking out a birthday gift for a friend. As I look through the racks of clothes, I chat with the woman helping me. She asks me what I'll do after graduation, and I tell her I'm waiting to hear back from law schools. "I have no idea where I'll be this time next year," I tell her, smiling. "California, New York, Pennsylvania…" Delicious ambiguity.

A few minutes later the phone rings. It's a 215 number, in the Philadelphia area code. "Hello?"

"Is this Jenna?" a woman asks.

"Yes, who's this?"

"It's Regina, from the office of admissions at Penn Law. Dean Post would like to speak with you."

My heart drops into my stomach. A minute later Dean Post gets on the phone. "Jenna," she says, "on behalf of Penn Law I would like to welcome you to the class of 2014."

I become disoriented and sit down on the chair closest to me. "I didn't actually think I was going to get in!" I say. Not the smartest thing to lead with, I know, but I am in total shock.

She laughs. "Well, after looking at your qualifications and…"

I got into Penn Law?! I can't believe it!

What if there had been no date party in October? What if David hadn't gone? What if David had never mentioned Penn Law? After planning for law school for years, I apply to Penn Law on a whim and get in two months later, almost to the day. In my mind, it's clear that G-d is directing me there for a reason.

When I check out at the store, I tell the woman helping me, "I just found out I'll be moving to Philadelphia next year."

CHAPTER 13

Doubt

January 2011

AT THE BEGINNING OF MY last semester of college, I get a call from a relative. We never speak outside of family gatherings. Why is he calling?

"I spoke with your grandma," he begins. "She said you're thinking of studying at an Orthodox school in Israel this summer."

"Yes, I am."

"Jenna, I feel a responsibility to tell you, you need to be aware of all the things you're going to give up if you become Orthodox. I have friends who are more observant. They can't go out to dinner with friends on Friday night, they can't go to the club on Saturday to play golf…"

Oh, the horror, I think. My relative is Conservative, has three children, and goes on vacation twice a year. He lives the classic American dream. I understand that in his world, Friday nights out with friends and Saturday golf are important. I already know that Shabbat dinner is a social sacrifice. I give up going out with my friends every week, but the tradeoff is worth it. And there's always Thursday or Saturday night.

He tells me the rabbis are rigid. That they create laws that make the Orthodox lifestyle very hard. "Ask your rabbi about rabbinic law," he says. "The laws take over your life. You are not going to have the freedom you have now."

I assure him that even if I go to Israel, I am not necessarily going to become Orthodox.

"That's what you say now," he says. "But once you're there, they have you."

"I am not joining a cult." Offended that he imagines I can't think for myself, I tell him I've been to Neve before and the rabbis don't pressure you into doing anything. On the contrary, they inspire you to *want* to observe the mitzvot.

"That's how it is in the beginning," he says. "Once you keep learning, you'll certainly feel the pressure to become more religious. They're investing time in you and they want to see results. They have agendas, these rabbis. What is their agenda? Ask your rabbi that too."

I think of the past months. Every Friday Rabbi Fleshel texts me: *Are you coming to Shabbat tonight?* Lately I can't tell if I say yes because I really want to go or because I feel like he expects me to. I've been meeting with him now once a week for a year and a half. He teaches me Torah and we schmooze about school, friends, family, life. I enjoy our learning and I know he cares about me, but it's obvious he wants me to go in a certain direction, a direction I'm not sure I want to go in. The Israel trip was a year and a half ago; I don't feel as inspired anymore.

I decide I need a break. I'm going to drop every Jewish thing I have taken on since the trip — Torah study, Shabbat dinner, candle lighting. If I come to it again on my own, I reason, then I will know this path is truly one that I choose.

CHAPTER 14

The Lost Princess

I MET ADAM[*] IN THE Writing Center during my freshman year. I had made an appointment with a writing instructor to go over one of my English papers, and he was my tutor that day. He came out of the instructors' lounge and looked at a few of us waiting.

"Jenna?" he called.

When I stood up, he smiled. He looked Jewish, with his shaggy brown, curly hair. He must have been at least a senior. I learned that he was a PhD student, getting his doctorate in philosophy.

We tried to stay focused on my paper, but kept going on personal tangents — music, classes, social life. It turned out he was Jewish.

I realized that if I wanted to actually get my papers edited in the future, I'd need to book another tutor at the Writing Center. But occasionally, over the years, we'd run into each other on campus and chat for a few minutes.

Soon after I decide to "take a break" from Judaism, I run into Adam on campus again. This time we talk for a while, and it is obvious there is chemistry. He asks for my number, and a few days later he calls and asks me out.

Our relationship progresses quickly, and before I know it, I am officially his girlfriend. Apparently, he liked me ever since the

---

[*] Name has been changed to protect privacy.

first day we met in the Writing Center, but he knew that I was too young for us to date then.

Every Friday night we go out for Indian food in Little Five Points, a grungy hipster neighborhood in Atlanta. I tell Adam how I used to go to Shabbat dinner every week, about my Israel trip, about Neve.

"If you keep dating me, Princess," he says with a smile, "you won't be going back to Neve." I laugh this off, but I know it's true.

"Stop calling me Princess," I tell him. Adam's taken to this term of endearment because of my Long Island upbringing. It makes me uncomfortable; I'm not the girly-girl type. And I've been trying to shed the JAP label since I got to Emory.

Adam, I've learned, is an atheist. I didn't realize it when we first started dating. I still believe in G-d, but I'm not so sure about Judaism anymore. I remember that sense of clarity I had in Israel almost two years before, but that's really all it is now, a memory.

Still, I expect Adam and I to discuss the nature of G-d and reality, especially given that he is a philosophy major. But he doesn't have much interest in engaging in these types of discussions. It turns out he gets enough philosophy in school.

When we do have deeper discussions, he tells me the most important thing in life is relationships with other people. He also believes in enjoying life as much as possible, a philosophy I know from experience can lead to hedonism, which does not appeal to me. In line with this philosophy, Adam wants an easy, stress-free life, which is why he plans to work in college administration, in a warm-weather climate, of course. I know he is capable of so much more.

"You know, I've been thinking," Adam says one day after a few months of dating, "about next year I. think I might apply to some jobs in Philadelphia."

I try to feign excitement, but all I feel is anxiety. When I'm alone, I realize that over the past couple of weeks I have begun to see how dark and empty a life without spirituality is. The absence of anything higher in my life now causes me again and again to come back to G-d. When I bring it up, though, I can tell Adam is turned off. I don't think I could marry someone who doesn't believe in G-d, who doesn't believe in anything.

Spring 2011

Spring break is coming up. As my friends get ready for Miami and Mexico, I get ready to go to Poland. Last semester, the rabbi got me on a coveted trip to Poland with Rabbi Shmuel Lynn from Penn, who made an exception and included me because I was starting Penn Law in the fall. I had always wanted to see the concentration camps for myself, to go back to the shtetl my grandparents' families had escaped.

A week before spring break, I come down with a bad cold. The thought of standing in freezing temperatures outside and confronting death is more than my body can handle. At the last minute, I change my plans and decide to stay with my grandma in Boca, where I can relax and recover in the warm Florida sun. Adam isn't happy, but I'm looking forward to having some space.

On the first Friday night of spring break, right before I leave for Florida, I meet Adam at his apartment, which is across the street from Chabad. That night, as I stand outside waiting for him, I notice the big tent behind their large, brick home. I hear students talking and laughing. I see the light emanating from the tent. I can almost smell the fresh challah.

The Indian restaurant in Little Five Points is small and loud. Waiters go by with plates of cheap, smelly Indian food. Flyers for bands hang on the wall. For the first time, I notice that one of them looks like a neo-Nazi band.

"Princess?" Adam says, trying to get my attention. "Princess?"

Normally when he calls me Princess, I become shy.

This time is different. I look at him. "You're right," I say, smiling. "I am a princess."

In that moment, something clicks. For the first time, I own the fact that I truly am a princess — a holy soul, a daughter of the King Himself.

I fight tears as I realize that my current life will never be enough. It is time for something more.

CHAPTER 15

Intervention

IN FLORIDA I SPEND A couple of days with my roommates, who are vacationing at the W Hotel in South Beach. We sit on sunbeds on the beach, tan, listen to music, and read magazines. Lying on the beach used to be one of my favorite pastimes, but I find it harder to enjoy now. In the absence of assignments and distractions, I am forced to confront myself. I feel anxious about the summer.

A month or two into dating Adam, I had told my friends and family that I wasn't going back to Neve after all, that I just want to relax before law school. My friends were relieved; they thought this whole seminary thing was crazy from the start. My parents, who did not want me going to Israel either, were more puzzled. They knew how badly I'd wanted this. "Okay," was all they said. But now that I'm "relaxing," I can't relax. What am I going to do this summer, sit around like this, day after day, until law school? A sense of emptiness has deepened in me since I stopped going to Shabbat dinner. I know I need to stop dating Adam.

Later that afternoon, as I drive up I-95 back to Boca, my phone rings. It's Cynthia.

I haven't seen Cynthia since the Israel trip, almost two years before. After the trip, we had decided to speak every first of the month. On our "Rosh Chodesh talks," as we called them, we'd relive our inspiration from the trip and discuss our spiritual growth since then. That only lasted for a short while, though. The last time we spoke was in the fall, before she went to work at the U.S. embassy in Argentina.

"Cynthia?" I answer.

"Jenna!" she says. "I was sitting on the beach meditating and your name literally popped into my head!"

"Where are you?" I ask.

"In Boca."

"Me too!"

"Are you serious?" she says. "I thought you were in school in Atlanta! I came home to help my mom, she had to have surgery. I'm leaving tomorrow, though, to go back to Argentina. Can we meet tonight?"

"Yes! I'll be home in an hour." We make plans to have dinner. I can't believe it.

That night, Cynthia and I catch up on the past year. She tells me about her work in Argentina, I tell her about Penn Law. We talk about our Jewish growth since the trip. She stays connected listening to Jewish classes online. I tell her about my learning with Rabbi Fleshel and my more recent decision to take a break from Judaism. I ask Cynthia what she's going to do after her stint at the embassy ends in May.

"I'm going back to Neve this summer," she tells me. "You have to come with me! We can be roommates!"

Immediately my defenses rush in to answer her: *What about their agenda? I don't know if I want to be Orthodox. I don't want to be brainwashed!* But once the initial fears and doubts subside, I can hear a quiet voice inside me saying: *The bottom line is, you saw a truth in Israel. You never got to the bottom of it. The teachers in Israel might have some answers. This is your last chance to really learn what it means to be Jewish.*

"Why shouldn't I go?" I hear myself say. Suddenly Adam and the rabbis and everything holding me back seem irrelevant. It's obvious to me that G-d has orchestrated my meeting with Cynthia that night. He is giving me another chance. I want to take it.

The day I get back to school from Florida, I break up with Adam. He tells me I'm making the biggest mistake of my life. When I leave his apartment I practically skip to my car, suddenly liberated, sure I've made the right decision.

The next day, the Monday that classes resume after spring break, my counselor Jackie from the Israel trip just "happens" to be in Atlanta, in part to connect with Emory students. We meet at the Hillel and I tell her how I've been struggling. I tell her I want to go to Neve for the summer with Cynthia.

"Jenna," she says, "if you think going to Israel is the right thing for you, you should act on it while you still have the clarity. When we have moments of clarity and inspiration, as you do now, you have to act on it right away. Otherwise, the doubts and fears can creep back in and paralyze you." I know she is right. That week, I book the flight that will take me back to Israel for the summer.

I inform my parents that I've decided to go to Neve after all to continue my Jewish studies.

"You're going back to Israel?" my mom exclaims. "What are you going to tell Grandpa?"

Grandpa. The hovering shadow.

Grandpa is not just unreligious, he is anti-religious. He once told me he wished he believed in G-d, which was actually the most religious thing I ever heard him say. Religion, he would say, gets in the way of success.

We have different metrics for how we view success, of course, but my grandpa can't understand this. Whenever I call him, the TV anchor fills the background with the latest market numbers.

He spends his days reviewing his stock portfolio for the tiniest error and speaks with his stockbroker as often as he speaks to my family, probably more. In his spare time, he likes to think of ways America could get out of its deficit. "Loan" is a word he loathes.

No, I decide, he won't know about this trip to Israel. During our weekly Sunday phone calls, which can happen from anywhere, I will engage him in conversation about the latest news, politics, my upcoming move to Philadelphia for law school — anything besides what is really in my heart.

CHAPTER 16

Back at Neve

Summer 2011

FROM THE MOMENT I AM back at Neve, it's hard to imagine I ever questioned a return. This trip is more personal, more intentional, and more focused than the last. I have one goal in mind: to look deeper into Judaism and determine if the Torah is in fact Divine.

Over the last two years, it has become clear to me more than ever that G-d — the force I formally referred to as a higher universal energy — exists. This truth feels more real and authentic to me than most anything else. Since the Israel trip two years ago, G-d and I have begun speaking to each other, and notwithstanding our occasional short breaks, it's an ongoing conversation. G-d speaks to me in a language only we can understand. He sends me signs, some small, and some not so small, like my one-night meeting with Cynthia earlier that year.

I feel that G-d's existence is part of my existence, part of my being. Yet I need to know that there is a legitimate logical basis for this feeling. Both for myself and to maintain my dignity in Western culture, where the only reality is the physical, logical one. I read books like *Permission to Believe*, by Rabbi Lawrence Kelemen, a Harvard graduate, and listen to classes by Rabbi Dr. Dovid Gottlieb, a former professor of philosophy at Johns Hopkins University. These teachers give me a solid rational foundation for a truth I feel intuitively, a truth that ultimately defies logic.

Still, there are many paths to serving G-d. If I am going to embrace Judaism as my path, then I need to make absolutely sure that the Torah is actually Divine, that it's the word of G-d. Otherwise, I am not going to change my entire life.

I'm not interested in the watered-down version of Judaism I experienced growing up, which was created to accommodate assimilation in Europe and America. I'm going for a true and deep spiritual path, whatever that is. For three thousand years, before the advent of Reform and then Conservative Judaism, "Orthodox" Judaism was the only Judaism. If the Torah is true, I tell myself, I am in all the way.

I begin each morning with a look into the Divine nature of the Hebrew language in Rabbi Marcus's class, The Mystical Hebrew Alphabet. Each letter, I learn, has a number and meaning. *Gematria* makes connections between letters or words with the same numerical value. For instance, the *alef* represents G-d's oneness. It is made up of a *vav* and two *yud*s. If those letters' numbers are added up, that makes twenty-six, which is the same numerical value as G-d's four-letter Name.

Connections between words are also made if they share the same root. For instance, I learn that the Hebrew word for love, *ahavah*, shares the same root letters, *hey* and *vet*, as the word for "give." From this, Rabbi Marcus tells us, we learn that one does not give to another because he loves him, but he comes to love the person because he gives to him. The giving precedes the love.

I would never think to make the connection between love and giving in this way. As I begin to see the Hebrew alphabet come alive, I realize why Hebrew is called *lashon hakodesh*, the holy tongue. In Hebrew, Rabbi Marcus explains, the word for "words" is *devar*, which also means "things." In Biblical Hebrew, an item's name reveals its essence. There is no arbitrary word, like "table," which could really mean anything, but we happen to ascribe it to mean table.

In our next class, Mitzvah and Meaning, with Rabbi Dovid Kass, we learn about the deeper meanings behind the mitzvot — which I learn doesn't just mean "good deeds," but "commandments," like keeping Shabbos, keeping kosher, and dressing modestly.

I learn about mitzvot that I didn't even know existed, like *lashon hara*, which literally means "evil tongue" and forbids speaking badly about another person or group of people. When my class first hears about the prohibition of *lashon hara*, we go into an uproar. As usual, we begin challenging and questioning. Our questions are welcomed, because in Jewish thought, one cannot really learn unless he questions. "But rabbi, what if we need to speak badly about someone because we need to vent?" or "What if we need to let someone know that so-and-so isn't a good person?" Rabbi Kass explains with his dry English humor that there are instances when one is permitted to speak *lashon hara* for a constructive purpose. I learn that the laws surrounding these instances are detailed and specific.

In fact, Jewish law is more intricate than I had ever imagined. Every action is regulated, down to the smallest detail. "Why does G-d care if I wash my right hand before my left before I eat bread?" I ask Rabbi Kass one day. "Does He really care about every little detail?"

"When you love someone," Rabbi Kass answers, "you show your love to him by noticing the details. His favorite color, his likes and dislikes. It's the same in our relationship with G-d. We want to show G-d we love Him by doing what He likes."

"But I don't understand," I say. "Is doing the mitzvot the only way to connect to G-d? The Jewish people make up such a small percentage of the world's population. Many other people claim a connection to the Divine, and they aren't doing mitzvot."

"Torah and mitzvot do not have a monopoly on connecting to G-d," Rabbi Kass replies, "but G-d designed the Torah and mitzvot to enable a more efficient, intense relationship with Him. Going back to the example earlier, if you want to have a connection with someone, you can do it pretty easily. But there's a difference between saying hello and buying someone their favorite candy; each act will create a different level of connection."

I allow this information to sink in. Even if I can't say for sure that the Torah is Divine, it seems worthy to try approaching Judaism this way, at least while I'm here. Maybe if I observe some of the mitzvot, I'll feel that the Torah is Divine. I can always stop doing it if I don't like it, I reason, so why not just try it out and see how it goes?

So, while I'm at Neve, I do as the religious do, for the most part. After all, the Torah literally means "teaching" or "instruction." It's meant to be lived, not just learned. I wear skirts and three-quarter-sleeve shirts to class. I keep kosher and I keep Shabbos. It's hard *not* to do these things at Neve.

Once I begin to experience Shabbos, I start to understand it. It is a true oasis in time. I discover that the restrictions of no phone, computer, or cars enable me to set myself free from the trappings of everyday life in the modern world, where things don't ever stop. I use the time to breathe, to reconnect to myself and G-d, and to process everything. Week after week, I look forward to Shabbos more and more.

One of the most popular classes at Neve is Rabbi Doniel Katz's. His class before lunch is shorter, about an hour and a half, but his afternoon class can go on for hours. In both classes, there is never an empty seat. Aside from questions and laughing at his occasional jokes, the room is silent as we take in the way Rabbi Katz reveals the Torah's depth and relevance beyond our wildest imagination.

Today before lunch, the small classroom is packed. Rows of girls sit behind desks, chatting as they wait for class to start. I take a seat next to Cynthia, who has recently decided that after her time at Neve, she will move to Israel and pursue her career in foreign diplomacy with a focus on Israel advocacy. Next to her is Sarah, who is a "Neve floater," which means she's been at Neve for so long that no one can keep track: Has it been two years? Did she finish college? It's not clear. She teaches Zumba to the girls on Tuesday nights in one of the dorm basements. In walks Talia, a wealthy Persian from LA in her early thirties. She came to Neve to take a break from life back home and maybe meet someone. I notice Nicole in the corner. She is an artist and splits her time between classes and her painting studio on campus. Thin colored markers sit neatly on her desk; she is poised to take notes as beautiful as the teachings we will hear.

The group of women at Neve is pretty diverse; mostly Americans and some "Anglos" from England, South Africa, or Australia. Most of the women are either in the middle of pursuing a college degree or recent graduates. There is a handful of women in their thirties, who woke up one day thinking, *Is this all there is? A successful career?* They're here for something more. We all are. We all stumbled onto Neve's enchanted campus as if falling through a rabbit hole, usually through an Israel trip. Some of us came here to escape our lives; others, like me, came here to enhance our lives.

I think how amazing it is that we've all chosen to take time out of "real life" to come to Israel to explore life's deepest questions. Even those who might have been fleeing from something at home rather than to something here are nonetheless poised for a transformation they would not likely get elsewhere. With the pressure from my family to pursue a high-powered law career, engaging in this kind of spiritual exploration is a luxury I can't afford for too long. I savor every moment, feeling blessed to be right here, in this small, crowded classroom.

Rabbi Katz enters, and we stand out of respect. He heads straight for the closet door, where he hangs his black hat and jacket. After he takes a seat at the desk in the front, he begins to stroke his long red beard and study his notes. The class grows quiet.

Finally, he says, "It is a misconception that you need something outside of yourself to complete yourself." And we're off.

"Every time you buy something with this mentality," he explains, "you reinforce this mentality. In truth, there is a point within yourself where you can feel so truly confident that you don't need an external thing or person to have total self-love."

I think about how much my identity growing up was connected to what clothing I wore, what cars my parents drove, what college I got into. How much of my identity is still tied to these things?

Rabbi Katz talks about healthy independence. About freeing ourselves from the things that distract us from our true selves, such as worrying about the future or thinking about the past. "Don't back out of things you are enjoying in the present because of worries of where it will lead you in the future," he says. That resonates with me. I've been enjoying learning at Neve for the past couple of weeks so much, but I can't let myself relax into it because I'm scared that if I do find that the Torah is true, then I'll have to change my whole life. I'll have to deal with my parents, my friends, Grandpa. How will I keep Shabbos in law school? Then I realize I'm doing exactly what Rabbi Katz has been speaking about: worrying about the future, which is taking me away from where I want to be in the present.

After class, I descend the stairs of the airy, light-filled main building and walk out into the serene paradise that is Neve's campus. Grassy lawns, filled with trees and sweet-smelling flowers, are surrounded by Jerusalem-stone buildings. It seems the sun is always shining and birds are always chirping. Sometimes I feel being here is just a dream. I walk down the narrow path that cuts through the lush campus to the cafeteria building. I notice one of the housemothers, with her long black skirt and short wig, standing outside her dorm. Her four small children run around her and play. "Hi," she says, smiling at me. "Are you new? What's your name?" We begin talking. I tell her that I'm from New York and that I just graduated college. She asks me how long I plan to stay at Neve.

"Just for the summer," I tell her. "I'm starting at Penn Law in the fall." For a moment I expect her to say, "Penn Law! Wow!" like my friends and family do back home.

Instead she says, "Very nice," but her words don't carry the same warm emotion she displayed just moments earlier. Unlike my family and friends at home, who are impressed by my admission to an Ivy League law school, I'm discovering that the teachers at Neve aren't really impressed at all. She glances away for a moment, "Yankele, I told you not to take Ruchie's doll!" Yankele doesn't listen, and she is forced to intervene. "It was nice to meet you," she says with a smile before darting after her children.

I am disconcerted. The religious people here don't understand what it takes to get into a school like Penn Law. Yet their anticlimactic responses humble me. As alien as Penn Law is to this woman, so the name Yankele is to me. I begin to realize that at Neve, people care more about who you are as a person and your good deeds than your career accomplishments. This realization is refreshing, but also unsettling. How much time have I invested in my career versus being a good person?

CHAPTER 17

Teshuvah

AFTER A FEW WEEKS AT Neve, I know what I have to do. After lunch, classes in the afternoon are optional, and everyone does their own thing. Today, as lunch is winding down, I make my exit.

I get up from the circle of women eating schnitzel and salad, talking and laughing outside on the grass. I walk down the narrow path to Building 4. Though it's hot, there's a slight breeze. I enter the code and immediately feel the AC upon entering the building. As I climb the stairs, I hear a door slam shut and then another door open. A girl passes me on the staircase, but other than that the building is empty. The natural light in the staircase dissipates as I enter our hallway. The walls are covered with inspirational signs and a chores rotation.

I unlock my door and lock it behind me. Cynthia and I each have a twin bed, with a desk and chair in between. Our closets are metal janitor closets. The white walls are pretty bare, and the room itself isn't so aesthetically pleasing, but it does the job. The best part is that my bed is next to a window that overlooks the Jerusalem hills. Around sunset or at night I love to sit and just look outside and breathe it all in.

I am not here to do that today. I put my bag and notebook down. I stand in front of the dresser facing east, where we're supposed to face when we pray. I take a deep breath. *Now what?* I think. Talk to G-d. *How do I do this?* Just try.

"Hi, G-d," I begin. "It's me, Jenna." I feel so stupid. Of course G-d knows who I am. He knows what I'm trying to do. I feel ridiculous standing in front of the janitor's closet. I force myself to continue, because despite how crazy I feel, I know I want this.

"I don't really know where to start." Exhale. There is so much. I am trying to do *teshuvah*, repentance.

One of my teachers at Neve, Rebbetzin Tziporah Heller-Gottlieb, explained that our souls are like a flame and our "sins" are like layers of garments wrapped around our souls. Our souls do not ever become tainted in their essence, she assured us. Our light may be dimmed, but it is never extinguished.

I remember Rabbi Katz's words from class. "First, admit that you did something wrong." Gulp. Most people who do *teshuvah* did one or two things wrong. I'm trying to unload a lifetime of wrongs.

I proceed to list everything I can remember that I've done wrong. The countless times I ate nonkosher food. One layer off. Being disrespectful to my parents. Another layer off. Driving on Shabbos. Another. Speaking gossip. Another. I include everything, but I focus on the times I "missed the mark" after I learned what the mark was. Before that, I really didn't know any better. Everyone ate nonkosher growing up. Everyone drove on Shabbos. Everyone wore shorts and skirts above the knees. We didn't think about those things.

"Second, really regret what you did."

I realize that I don't really regret most of the things I did. All the salads I ate at the Whole Foods salad bar that were not checked properly under Jewish law? I enjoyed those salads. They were healthy and convenient when I was in finals. My pants? I love wearing pants. It feels like me. I go on like this. Finally I stop myself. If I don't regret the things I did, why do I feel a deep sense of pain and regret? Because I regret that I did things that G-d didn't want me to do.

I had just learned that G-d wants a relationship with us. That when we love someone, we do what he wants to make him happy. It's the same with G-d. It hurt me that I was doing things that G-d didn't want, that I was hurting Him, so to speak.

"G-d," I whisper, "I regret that what I did went against Your will and put distance between us." Now, that's an honest statement. I make myself sit in this regret for a while. I rock back and forth and tears come to my eyes. *I want a fresh start*, I keep thinking. *I want a fresh start.*

"Next, make a plan not to repeat what you did."

Initial panic sets in again. I can't never wear pants again. I can't promise that I will never eat nonkosher food again. I want to eventually never do those things again, but if I take on these commitments all at once, it's not going to be real.

"G-d, I can't promise that I won't do these things again. But I'll never do them again with the same lightheartedness. I'll know the implications of my actions. I want to keep Your Torah properly, but I need time to get there in a healthy way. Please be patient with me." As I hear myself say these words, I immediately feel calmer and surrounded by love. I also know that I've crossed over some sort of threshold and my life will never be the same.

"Last, ask for forgiveness."

"G-d, please forgive me. Forgive me. Forgive me. Forgive me." I am pleading now. "I am so sorry. I didn't know any better. I know now. I love You, please." I am swaying back and forth, my lips are wet, and I can taste my tears. I feel like G-d is hugging me and saying, "It's okay. I know. Don't worry."

As I open my eyes, I expect everything around me to look different. The janitor's closet stares me in the face. The beds, half-made, haven't changed. The blank walls mutely bear witness to what just occurred.

It is me who has changed.

CHAPTER 18

In the Light, Look for the Truth

ONE DAY AT LUNCH I walk over to a group of girls sitting on the lawn in front of the cafeteria and join them. Neve is a big place with several schools within it, so there are always new faces. It turns out that one of the girls, Rachel, grew up in the same area I did. She went to one of the Jewish day schools in the Five Towns area and is now a counselor for another Neve program. We exchange numbers. I'm happy to have a contact for when I go home, but I don't think much of it; I need to go get a seat in Rabbi Katz's afternoon class.

Today Rabbi Katz is teaching about *emunah*, faith, and *emes*, truth.

Life, he explains, is a flow between clarity and doubt. We have times of light, when everything is so clear and we're happy and things are going well. Then we have times of darkness, where there is pain, challenges, and suffering. Why? Because only in those times of darkness, when things aren't so clear, can you really exercise free will, he tells us. Only in those times of challenge can you really *choose* G-d, choose to continue living according to your values.

Rabbi Katz reminds me of a teaching I heard from Rabbi Tatz: Faith in Judaism is not blind faith; it is being faithful to what you know intellectually to be true.

Jews exist to bring light into the darkness, Rabbi Katz explains, to elevate the physical world into the spiritual by making a place for G-d here in this world. G-d is with you in the lowest place, he tells us, because He wants you to find Him even there.

I think about that morning in the Bahamas. *G-d is with you in the lowest place because He wants you to find Him even there.*

When you actively choose good, Rabbi Katz says, that choice becomes you. The inspiration is now part of your being; you have internalized it. That's why we need to learn about light in this world *through* darkness. In the darkness, our will is awakened, and choosing good in that state brings us to a more powerful, permanent light.

I remember my first Israel trip. I was basking in light, high on Torah learning. Then, back at Emory, I was in the dark. I became confused and forgot what I had learned that felt so true. By the time I made the choice to come back to Neve this summer, I was hanging on by a thread. Still, I had chosen good.

Now, I realize, the pattern is repeating on a larger scale. At Neve I'm in a place of light. It's clear that there is a G-d. At this point, after more than a month of learning full-time, it is even clear to me that the Torah is Divine.

I have taken Rabbi Kelemen's class based on his book *Permission to Receive: Four Rational Approaches to the Torah's Divine Origin*, where he uses history of religion and statistics to show that Judaism is the only religion that claims a mass revelation, meaning that G-d spoke to more than one person (three million!) at one time at Mount Sinai. This is a hard revelation narrative to withstand 3,500 years, he explains. It's much easier to claim one person heard G-d speak, because it cannot be verified. To claim that three million people heard G-d speak can certainly be verified — or more likely discredited — at the time the narrative is born. Yet this claim has endured for thousands of years.

I also believe that the miraculous nature of Jewish survival throughout history is proof of the Torah's Divinity. The Torah is called the blueprint of reality, and Jewish history has reflected the

Torah's blueprint. When the Jewish people observed G-d's commandments, the blessings He promised us in the Torah came to be. When we did not, the curses that G-d warned us of also occurred. The Torah says that the Jewish people will inherit the Land of Israel. That we will go into exile yet remain a nation eternally. Despite all odds, this has also happened. The remarkable survival and thriving of the Jewish people is not only acknowledged by Jews. As Mark Twain wrote in his famous "Concerning the Jews" essay, "All things are mortal but the Jew; all other forces pass, but he remains. What is the secret of his immortality?"

Though I find these and other similar arguments convincing, my understanding of the Torah's Divinity has come naturally through immersing myself in its teachings. The Torah itself is the greatest proof of its authenticity. Its depth is supernatural, beyond that of men's finite understanding. In my mind, no man or group of men could have conceived writings with such depth and perfect wisdom of human nature and the world around us. I feel that to claim that men wrote the Torah is like saying that men filled the ocean themselves. The Torah, in its entirety, is simply beyond us. It's hard to appreciate this point without really studying it for yourself.

That's not to say I still don't have some personal hang-ups to resolve about Orthodox Judaism — for one, the Torah's view on climate change and environmentalism. Even though I've learned that the Torah has many mitzvot that encourage environmental protection, I have not seen this ethic demonstrated in the religious communities I've visited. I'm also nervous about the role of women in Judaism. Although I know that it's acceptable for women to have a career — and also that secular studies can be valued for their own wisdom and insight — the priority is the home. Will I be forced to sacrifice my career ambitions if I become a religious woman? I definitely have not worked everything out, but by now I've learned enough to know that the wisdom in the Torah is true.

Whatever my personal hang-ups, they do not alter the fact that I am first and foremost obligated to observe the Torah.

In the darkness, Rabbi Katz teaches, you will be tested. Your feelings will cloud your judgment and you will want to choose personal convenience over your desire to keep Hashem's Torah. In these instances, Rabbi Katz advises us, hold on to the intellect. "In the light, look for the truth, and in the dark, stay true to the light." I write that down.

I am in a place of light. Keeping kosher and Shabbos at Neve is easy. I wake up inspired to learn Torah. This inspiration is inherent to seminary, but it's external to me. Soon I'm going to leave the Holy Land and go to a place of spiritual darkness. It will not be easy or convenient to keep kosher in my parents' house or observe Shabbos at Penn Law School. Yet only there can I really choose G-d, can I really *choose* to keep the Torah. Once I make that choice, then the light of the Torah will become a part of me.

I came to Neve to find truth, and as scary as it is to admit it, I think I have found it. I tell myself that I need to stay true to the light, to the Torah, when I go back home and make it real for myself. These words will be my armor, my shield.

Still, I'm nervous. I know I need a plan. I meet with Jackie, and she helps me decide which mitzvot I will keep no matter what when I go home. A bare minimum, so to speak, to keep me connected:

- Lighting Shabbos candles
- Making Kiddush on Shabbos
- Not using the phone or computer on Shabbos
- Saying morning blessings, the bedtime Shema, and praying in my own words each morning
- Keeping kosher in my apartment at law school
- Learning Torah once a week
- Finding myself a rabbi or mentor in Philly

Before I leave Israel, I also write myself a letter to bottle a bit of the light I'm experiencing, so that I might refer to it in darker times:

Jenna,

Now is the time to make the truth real and part of your reality. I know it might be hard to stay connected, but keep fighting and then you'll have it! Do not go below the "minimum" — keep learning and keep Shabbos and you will connect. Remember, don't feel guilty, but happy in where you are holding. The important part is which direction you're moving in. You may feel that schoolwork comes first, but your connection with G-d does. Go forward in what you know to be true and be strong... Stay true to the light in the dark and come back to Israel for more learning. (You want a Torah-learned husband!)

Love,

Me

I want to stay at Neve and defer law school for the year, but I know before even mentioning it to my parents that it will never fly with Grandpa. To spend a year investing in my values and spiritual growth does not contribute to my financial success in any way, and the latter is all that matters in my grandpa's world.

I have not explicitly told my parents that I've decided to observe the Torah. Still, in an attempt to assert my independence and newfound identity, I alert them that one day I will return to Israel and continue my studies, even if it's after law school. My parents reluctantly agree, banking on the probability that it will never happen.

It's finally time to leave Neve. My friends walk me to the gate at the bottom of the hill to say goodbye. As the sun sets, the *sherut* van comes right on time. Before I know it, I'm looking out the window at my friends waving, tears streaming down my face. I am not the first Jew to cry because I must leave Israel.

On the plane, I look through the Neve yearbook that we got at the final banquet. Each teacher has a quote to impart to the students. I cannot believe my eyes when I read Jackie's words of wisdom: *The road to growth can only begin with the realization that you are a princess.* I can't believe it! I remember that Friday night in the Indian restaurant when I told Adam he was right, that I was a princess, a daughter of the King. I didn't belong in that grungy restaurant on a Friday night. This realization helped propel me back to Neve.

I never told Jackie that. I feel G-d is winking at me.

Part II
STRUGGLE

CHAPTER 19

I Gave Birth to My Grandmother!

MY MOM OPENS THE FRONT door to greet me and finds me wearing a long black skirt. To wear only skirts from now on is not on my list of "must keeps," but I want my parents to understand that I have changed.

"What are you wearing?" She laughs. "You look like you walked out of the shtetl!" I remind her that we had bought this black maxi skirt together before I left. She thought I was going to wear it only in Israel, out of respect for the rabbis.

My mom grew up with little formal Jewish education and observance, but her grandparents were from the shtetls of Poland and often spoke Yiddish. Mama and Papa, as they were lovingly called, infused my mom with a warm Jewish feeling, so my mother can understand my wanting to embrace Judaism, but only to a point. After all, I'm deviating from the plan to be a hardworking, successful lawyer in New York City, married to a rich Jewish professional, and wearing Tory Burch flats while doing it. We are supposed to be Reform, but if necessary, Conservative is okay too. Don't I understand?

I try to explain that I can't just pick and choose religion; I've studied the Torah and determined that there's a strong probability that it's a Divine text, certainly great enough to observe it.

"Give me a break, Jenna," my mom says. "The Torah was written by a group of men who wanted to suppress women."

"Mom — you're making statements based on your impressions, rather than anything you actually know. You haven't studied Torah, so how can you say anything about it?" I try to control my frustration as I remember the classes we had on respecting our parents. The teachers warned us that returning home to our parents might be challenging. I didn't think I would have to face the challenge head-on from the moment I got off the plane.

I take a deep breath and start over. "Mom. All I'm doing is adding to the values that you and Dad gave me." This was a line one of the rabbis told us might be useful when returning home.

"Jenna, don't give me that line the rabbis fed you," my mom answers. I suppress my laugh. "I just don't understand why a girl like you, who is pretty, smart, and has so much potential, wants to live a life of such restriction."

Her statement is not really a question, but I answer anyway. I explain that I've learned that true freedom isn't just doing whatever you want, which is really a kind of enslavement to your desires that doesn't usually end well. But my words fall on deaf ears.

"I feel like I gave birth to my grandmother," she replies. We both laugh. Mama's name was Faigel Rochel, or Fanny, as she was called in America. Mama wanted to be religious. She lit Shabbos candles every Friday night. Yet my great-grandpa was willing to go only so far. That and the tide of assimilation kept her observance at bay.

"You'll never find a guy with those long, slim legs covered in a skirt," my mom warns me as she heads into the kitchen. "Forget about it."

I let out a chuckle and roll my eyes.

CHAPTER 20

Back in America

Late Summer 2011

I SPEND MY FIRST SHABBOS back in America sitting home alone, reading all day while my parents go about their errands. After two weeks of this, I realize I need a support system. Through my teachers at Neve, I get connected with the Blumsteins, the rabbi and rebbetzin of the Young Israel of Hewlett at the time, which is the closest Orthodox shul to my home.

I tell my parents I'm going to spend Shabbos with the Blumsteins, but they balk at the idea of my sleeping in a stranger's house. In religious circles, I explain, it's perfectly normal to stay at someone's home for Shabbos. Still, to help them ease into the transition of my new Shabbos observance, I decide to go for just Friday night dinner and then walk home. Mrs. Blumstein encourages me to invite my parents; only my dad accepts.

That Friday night I light the Shabbos candles at home, and then it starts to rain, hard. I'm undeterred. I need to prove to G-d, to my parents, and to myself that I am for real. That the commitments I made are solid. I leave the house in just a raincoat and rain boots, since umbrellas are not allowed on Shabbos, and I obviously cannot drive. My dad will join me there. As I feel the steady raindrops on my coat, with a half-hour walk in front of me, I hear my mom yell from the front door, "You're crazy!"

I walk in the rain down the long, winding streets. I begin to question myself. Maybe I am crazy. Then I remember Rabbi Katz: *You can only choose G-d in the dark. In the dark, stay true to the light.* I show up at the rabbi's house sopping wet, feeling like a refugee. They welcome me warmly and give me dry clothes to change into. The Blumsteins have eleven children. They're all there tonight, plus some of the older children's spouses and their children. Each person introduces himself, but it's hard to keep their names straight. Everyone is doing their own thing; some are in the kitchen, helping the rebbetzin prepare the meal. Some kids run around and play, while others sit around the living room and talk. When my dad arrives, we settle on a couch. My dad politely replies to the family's warm attempt to get to know him, but I know he feels totally out of place. Religion makes him uncomfortable. Just being around religious people makes him feel uncomfortable.

As assimilated as my mom's family is, my dad's family is even more so. My dad's maternal grandparents, my great-grandparents, were assimilated Americans. His family had their Passover Seders at Tavern on the Green, an iconic, upscale restaurant in Central Park, although certainly not kosher. Several relatives chose to be cremated. My father, like me, grew up attending Temple Israel of Lawrence but not connecting to it.

A child of the sixties, my dad went through his own spiritual journey, but it did not include Judaism, and so he feels alienated by my new path. He doesn't challenge it as intensely as my mother does, but he just doesn't understand it.

His alienation hurts, because my dad and I have always been on the same page. We understand each other on a level few parents and children are lucky enough to experience. Perhaps it's because we have led parallel lives in many ways: growing up in the same house, in the same area, going to the same Hebrew school yet never feeling like we really fit in. We both love music. We both love down-to-earth honesty. We get turned off by excess materialism and showy people. Whenever I'm home, we often stay up late, talking for hours. We laugh at the absurdity of people, of life. We strip down the world we're living in and the issues we're dealing with in a way that we can do only at night when we aren't pressured by daytime responsibilities and can see things for what they really are.

During our late-night talks, when my mom is fast asleep in their room with the TV on, I begin telling my dad what it is about Torah that I find so inspiring. I peel back the loaded term "Orthodox." I explain what's going on behind the images of the men in black hats and the women in wigs driving minivans around town. The Torah is a guidebook to reality, I tell him, to living the best possible life. The mitzvot are not burdens but spiritual opportunities to connect to G-d. That's why I'm trying to observe them. I explain that Judaism is a spiritual path that encourages engaging in the physical world and elevating it, and that through spiritual growth in this way one can achieve a lasting "high," a connection to G-d, that's natural. My dad starts to get it. "You explain it so well," he tells me.

Yet in the morning he forgets. Light, darkness. Clarity, confusion. He continues to side with my mom: I'm going too far. I understand; they don't want to lose me.

We sit at the Blumsteins' table, surrounded by their large family. As we pass the kugel and chicken around and listen to the family's discussion, I think more about how there is something about Jewish people being around more observant Jews that can make them feel uncomfortable or guilty or both.

I experience this after coming back from Neve when I meet up with friends. Some encourage me and find what I'm doing intriguing. They ask me questions as if looking into an aquarium tank: curious and engaged but distant. They act as if my spiritual growth has nothing to do with them, even though they are Jews too. They manage a certain cognitive dissonance. Others can't manage this dissonance and so ignore the subject of my newfound observance altogether, acting as if it doesn't exist. Or else they're just not interested. Regardless, it's hard for me to take. I'm going through a profound inner shift, and it's like my emerging self is irrelevant.

I get it, though. My spiritual growth forces them to think: *Should I look into this Judaism thing?* Many people don't choose to grow or take on responsibility in this way.

I'm proud of my dad for stepping out of his comfort zone. I'm also proud of myself. I hover between two worlds, neither of which is completely comfortable at the moment: my parents' home, with its nonkosher kitchen and the phone ringing off the hook on Shabbos, and the Blumsteins, as lovely as they are, with their eleven kids.

After the meal, my dad offers me a ride home. As he gets into the car alone, the significance of the moment seeps in. My newfound observance is separating us. His pain is palpable when he says, "I'll see you at the house."

The rabbi and rebbetzin offer to walk home with me. I assure them that the rain has stopped and I'll be okay, though I really do want their company. The way home is a long enough walk for me to get stuck in my own head, and I need distraction. They insist, so I relent.

We start out, me beside the rebbetzin with the rabbi beside her. I share with them a bit about my past, my fears, and hopes for the future. I want their insights on growing spiritually in a Jewish way. This conversation occupies us for some time, as we walk farther away from where the religious community lives and deeper into my neighboring nonreligious neighborhood.

We walk past the manicured lawns, hearing nothing but our own voices, insects, and the occasional passing car. Then a few drops start to fall. *Oh no,* I think. We're still about twenty minutes from my house. At least we're wearing raincoats.

I know my parents are waiting for me. I imagine my mom

watching TV and my dad listening to music in his sitting room. The rain becomes a steady drizzle. I imagine how my parents will react when I get home. They probably hear the rain and are worried. In high school, my mom wouldn't go to sleep until I walked in the door; it drove me crazy. We quicken our pace. I wish we could get there already. I wonder if the rabbi and rebbetzin want to turn back. I wish my family kept Shabbos.

We pass SKA, the large red-brick Orthodox Jewish high school for girls, tucked away on a private estate. I had driven by the school countless times growing up and never paid it much thought. Now I find myself wishing that I had gone there instead; that I received a real Jewish education.

We keep walking. We grow quiet and look down to shield excess rain from our faces. My hands, dry and warm in my jacket pockets, fiddle with my house key.

I tell the rabbi and his wife that they can turn back whenever they want, but they seem determined to escort me home. And so, we keep going for what seems like forever, in and out of conversation, raindrops cascading harder and heavier, until we reach the corner of my street. By now it's pouring so hard I can hardly see their faces as I turn to wave goodbye before running into my house.

When I close the door behind me, I expect to hear my parents call my name from their bedroom, summoning me for a lecture. Instead, all I hear is their TV from upstairs. I hang my soaked jacket on a chair in the entryway and tiptoe upstairs as quietly as I can, past their closed door, down the hall, and into my room. I sigh with relief, safe for now. I hear the rain pounding on the roof. I look in the mirror at my drowned-rat self and thank G-d that my parents fell asleep.

As I get into bed in my warm, dry pajamas, I think of the rabbi and his wife and their half-hour walk home, two lights in the dark streets. I can't believe the kindness of these people, the level of generosity they showed me tonight. I never experienced such giving from people outside my own family. I feel guilty to be inside, cozy in my bed listening to the rain fall, while they are still wet and cold outside. But I know that really, they are the lucky ones.

CHAPTER 21

Making Connections

I HAD NEVER HEARD OF Tishah B'Av before. As Rabbi Katz explained in class, this is exactly why we are in mourning. Jews are so deep in exile that we don't even realize we are in exile.

I try to fast but break it by midday. I figure I did well, given that I'd never heard of this day before. I get a text from Rachel, the girl I met at Neve who is also from the Five Towns. I had totally forgotten this connection.

"Do you want to come to my aunt's to break your fast later?"

I feel strange accepting the invitation, since I have just broken the fast, but I'm desperate to meet more religious people in the area.

Rachel's aunt lives a ten-minute drive from my house. On my way there, I'm nervous. I expect her to be somber and religious. She will doubtless be polite, but I fear there will inevitably be a barrier of connection between us because of our different backgrounds.

When I arrive, the house is filled with the smell of vegetable soup. Illana, Rachel's aunt, comes to greet me. She is beautiful: fair skin, dark hair, and warm, sparkling eyes. She smiles and welcomes me as she goes about preparing the meal, tired from a long day of fasting. I sit in the booth of the kitchen table while she, Rachel, and Rachel's friend Tanya finish preparing the meal. Illana's youngest daughter, Nava, about five years old, comes downstairs. She is fair-skinned like her mother, but with lighter brown hair and glasses.

The Moskowitzes, I learn, have another daughter, fifteen-year-old Aliza, who is away in Israel for the summer.

I feel comfortable immediately. But it's more than comfort; I feel I've been here before. That I have met Illana before. It's a strange feeling and it overwhelms me.

When Illana's husband, Keith, comes home, we start the meal. Keith has the fairest complexion of all, with light blond hair. He is soft-spoken and warm. Over the meal, I tell the Moskowitzes my story. They listen intently, their eyes wide as I describe how I fell in love with Torah and how I have been struggling since I got home.

They're inspired by my story, but it isn't foreign to them. It turns out that Keith did not grow up religious, and though Illana grew up traditional, she became more observant over time.

"You're welcome here anytime for Shabbos," Illana tells me. "Seriously." She gives me her number.

That weekend I planned to go to the Hamptons for a close friend's birthday party. Somehow, I think I'm going to keep Shabbos on my own over the weekend. After a lot of deliberating, I admit to myself that my friend's Hamptons house is not the best environment for keeping Shabbos. I muster the courage to call Illana and ask if I can take her up on her invitation. She welcomes me with open arms, inviting me to stay in Aliza's room while she is away.

Throughout my Shabbos at the Moskowitzes, I feel at home and at ease. Illana and I talk about anything and everything. She has a wonderful sense of humor and great confidence — she does what works for her, regardless of others' expectations. I like that. On Shabbos morning, we sit on the couch in our pajamas while Keith is at shul. I tell Illana what is really going on at home, how I'm struggling to make Torah observance a part of me. We laugh about how ridiculous I must seem to my parents. "You're a crazy religious freak," she tells me, joking. Then we get serious. She gives me advice about dealing with my parents in a respectful way. This is the first time I really feel understood since coming back from Israel. It's a huge relief.

I spend the next Shabbos with the Moskowitzes again. This time they take me with them to their shul, Aish Kodesh, on Friday night. When I refer to Aish Kodesh as "temple," Illana corrects me; apparently, Jews aren't supposed to call shuls temples, because we do not have the Temple in Jerusalem. I learn that Aish Kodesh, which literally means "the holy fire," is named after a chassidic Rebbe, the Piaseczna Rebbe, who was murdered in the Holocaust.

Illana tells me how in the Warsaw Ghetto, when the world was burning down around them, the Rebbe remained sane and strong, an anchor for his community. He secretly spoke *divrei Torah*, words of Torah, every Shabbos, to strengthen and encourage those around him. He transcribed these speeches and hid them in the ghetto. They were later discovered and published into a book called *Aish Kodesh* (The Holy Fire), which is how the Rebbe got this nickname. When the Rebbe and the remaining Jews in Warsaw were transported to the Trawniki work camp, the revered religious leader had an opportunity to escape the death trap he found himself in but chose to remain with his community. He was murdered along with his fellow Jews in the gas chambers of Treblinka, but not before he led them in saying the Shema.

Aish Kodesh is majestic and imposing. Keith explains that the wood-carved doors are a replica of those in the famous pre-World War II Rema shul in Krakow. When I walk into the lobby, I notice a large mural of the Warsaw Ghetto on the left wall.

There are two doors to the sanctuary: Keith heads to the men's section and Illana and I go to the women's, which is separated by a rich, dark-wood partition with sheer curtains. The women's section is a fraction of the size of the men's, but I learn this is because women are not obligated to come to shul and so need less space.

Indeed, there are many fewer women than men tonight, and we have plenty of room.

I open my siddur and turn to the Shabbos section. I don't know Hebrew and am still learning the prayers. I notice Jews from all spectrums of the Orthodox community here: men in black velvet *kippahs*, white knitted kippahs, black hats, and even *shtreimels*, the round fur hats worn by some chassidim. I've never seen anything like it before. In a large Jewish community like the Five Towns, there are many shuls for each type of Jew, so it's rare to find a group so diverse.

The shul begins to sing "*Yedid Nefesh*," a love song offered by the Jewish people to G-d, and its beautiful, melodic tone brings tears to my eyes as I follow along in English. "Majestic, beautiful, radiance of the universe, my soul pines for Your love…"

Throughout the song I realize that despite the mix of Jews here, everyone is united in their desire for a real, meaningful connection to G-d. The singing is so powerful because you can hear the voice of people who, despite whatever they are going through, are reaching out to G-d and yearning to connect to Him. As one journalist who observed the shul wrote, "Hope and despair intermingle here, or perhaps more accurately, hope seems to conquer despair and raise it to the higher celestial spheres. Where pure, unadulterated faith reigns supreme, everything is possible."

Illana guides me through the service, showing me which part we are up to. I try to read some of the prayers on my own in English. Then the congregation sings "*Lecha Dodi*," the pinnacle of the service welcoming the Shabbos. When the song is over, everyone continues singing the tune, without the words, the melody elevating higher and higher. Some people are swaying, others are rocking. Their eyes are closed, holding their prayer books close as they sing. It goes on like this for a while. A wordless song from the depths of the heart, I realize, conveys an emotion far beyond words.

After the service, Rabbi Moshe Weinberger stands in front of the intricately carved wooden ark housing the Torah scrolls. The ark nearly reaches the ceiling. He wears a *shtreimel* and a long black silk jacket, almost a coat. His garb is similar to that of some chassidim.

"Good Shabbos," he says, in a strong, warm voice, using the traditional Ashkenazi pronunciation.

"Good Shabbos," the community answers.

Rabbi Weinberger speaks in a mix of English, Hebrew, and Yiddish. I can't understand everything he says, but Illana translates for me.

"Being a Jew," he says, "doesn't mean only going to prayer services and keeping Shabbos, which of course is wonderful. Being a Jew means having closeness to Hashem… It's connecting to Hashem using the full spectrum of one's emotional and intellectual faculties."

It is clear why Rav Weinberger, as I learn he is called, named the shul Aish Kodesh, the Holy Fire. He seeks to ignite the flame in each Jew to have a deep connection to G-d and Torah. This may sound straightforward, but in any organized religion with many rituals, it becomes easy to merely go through the motions. The flame in a Jew, I learned at Neve, never goes out, but it needs "wood," or sustenance, to keep it alive. Rav Weinberger's Torah and the singing at Aish Kodesh is that wood, which is why hundreds of people pack into the shul each Friday night.

After just one visit to Aish Kodesh, I know I have found my spiritual home in New York, just ten minutes' drive from my parents' house and a five-minute drive from our old house on Clubhouse Road.

CHAPTER 22

"Get in the Car"

THE NEXT FRIDAY AFTERNOON, AS I pack my things into a bag, I assure my mom several times that I will call her right after Shabbos. "Going to sleep in a stranger's house — who heard of such a thing?" she says. Even though Illana has reached out to my mom and introduced herself, my mom still feels uneasy about the whole arrangement.

My parents have bought tickets to a Bob Dylan concert the following night, which starts before Shabbos ends. They want me to come with them, but that would mean getting into a car and breaking Shabbos. I insist that I'll meet them at the concert after Shabbos. But my mom is worried about my driving there alone, because it's supposed to rain (classic Jewish-mother syndrome). I give her Illana's address "just in case" and fly out the door to make it in time for candle lighting.

I replay this scene as Illana and I walk to her sister Leah's house late on Shabbos afternoon the next day. As we get closer, I can smell salt from the bay. A cool breeze from the water is a relief in the New York summer humidity. I hear birds chirping and sounds of construction from a nearby house. We pass kids playing basketball, running around and laughing. A couple pushing a baby in a stroller walks past us, and we wish each other good Shabbos.

As we walk up Leah's driveway, I hear a car drive up behind us over the crackling stones. It is my dad's black truck. I feel a rush of excitement; I miss them. I assume they are coming to say hi. I can't believe they tracked us down here. My dad rolls down the window and my mom leans over him. "Jenna, get in the car," she announces. "It's supposed to rain tonight, we don't want you driving to the concert alone."

I stand there in disbelief. My silence only angers my mom. She picks up a newspaper and waves it at me. "It's past sunset, we checked the time." Though my heart is racing, I want to laugh. They don't realize that Shabbos ends at least an hour after sunset. "I can't. I'm sorry," I say. Silence. "Please, don't do this to me," I plead softly. Illana looks at me. I can tell she wants to help but feels uncomfortable; she hardly knows my parents. She shifts her feet and I look down and back up at my parents.

I know this is a test. I remember Rabbi Katz's words: *In the dark, stay true to the light.* Growing impatient, my dad rolls his eyes and tilts his head back and I can see the lines on my mom's forehead as she insists, "Jenna, get in the car. Just get in!"

"Get in the car," my dad repeats. The car is the divider of our respective worlds. In my world, it's Shabbos. In theirs, it's Saturday. They're forcing me to choose between them and G-d. I begin to choke up. "Please. I can't. I'll meet you at the concert. Don't worry, it will be fine." But to them it isn't fine. I am rejecting the life they taught me. I really want to say, *I love you. I'm sorry closeness to G-d seems to be separating us. I wish I could just be the person you want me to be and be happy with that. But I'm going my own way and I'm scared. Why can't you trust me to find myself without judgment and make this a bit easier?*

But I don't say any of that. And after more back-and-forth, they drive away angry, confused, and upset. My stomach tightens and my heart hurts; I can't believe they think I *want* to create distance between us. And even though I am fighting tears, I know I've done the right thing.

As soon as Shabbos is over, I jump into my car and rush to the concert. When I enter the outdoor amphitheater, I see a frail man with a guitar onstage, sitting on a stool. Bob Dylan's raspy voice fills the stadium, illuminated by stage lights. My parents, along with everyone else, sit and watch, nodding along to the music. But when I get closer, I can see they're stiffer than usual, staring blankly at the stage, their faces revealing that they aren't really enjoying anything at the moment. I join them and squirm in my seat, glancing between them and the stage. I want to say something that will make it okay, but I realize that, at that moment, my words are useless.

CHAPTER 23

Grandpa's Visit

IN THE FINAL WEEKS BEFORE law school, Grandpa comes for his annual end-of-August visit to New York. Even at the age of ninety-five, he insists on flying alone.

My parents have spent the last week cleaning up the house, tidying and organizing and getting rid of excess clutter in anticipation of his visit. Despite their best efforts, the house always seems to be overflowing with too much stuff, according to my grandpa.

I decide to spend Shabbos at home, so as not to arouse his suspicion. When he first arrives, I'm careful not to wear a skirt. On Shabbos, I wear a shorter, form-fitting skirt, but I'm not too worried; women in my grandpa's day traditionally wore skirts, and the men wore suits and hats. To think of it, everyone dressed in a modest, dignified manner then, not unlike how many Orthodox Jews dress.

On Shabbos day, Grandpa limps his way into the kitchen. He walks as fast as possible in an attempt to mask his inability to get around like he used to. He sits in my dad's chair at the head of the table. He puts on his large-framed glasses, ancient things from the seventies, and begins to read the paper. "Jenna," he says without looking up, "do you know how to make coffee?" Really he is saying, *All respectable women should know how to make coffee.* Actually, I don't. I am a tea drinker. Fortunately, my parents made coffee before they left to run some errands, so all I have to do is pour some into a mug and bring it over. He nods as I place it on the table before him.

"Can you make me a sandwich?" he asks.

"What kind of sandwich?"

"Turkey and cheese."

I walk over to the fridge and take the turkey out of the drawer, which is right next to the cheese. "We're out of cheese," I tell him. I know he would never go looking in the fridge himself. Gentlemen don't fix their own food. Thankfully, he is happy with plain turkey and mustard.

"Toast it for me," he says. I know I'm not supposed to use a toaster on Shabbos. I stare at the toaster and back at my grandpa, his manicured hands holding the paper, oblivious to the reality of Shabbos.

I remind myself of my minimal observance commitment: lighting candles; no TV, phone, or computer; and making Kiddush. I lift the thick black cord of the toaster, unplugged as per my parents' habit when an appliance is not in use, and as I plug it into the wall my heart sinks.

I sit with Grandpa at the table as he eats his lunch. Soon he will go outside to read in the backyard and I can make Kiddush and say the blessing over the bread and have a Shabbos meal. He puts down his paper and looks up at me. "I've been looking around the house, over here, and there's too much stuff." I nod, as if in agreement.

"The family's spending is out of control," he says. "The bathroom has six, seven bottles of soap in the shower." I nod sympathetically, though I have heard this all before. On Grandpa's last visit, he sat my family down in the living room and proceeded to lecture us for "wasting our money on toiletries." If my mom were a cat, her tail would have shot straight up in the back. It took every ounce of her being to hold her tongue. My dad and I looked at each other, exchanging quick smiles. We wanted to laugh, it was so absurd.

As he eats his lunch, I try to change the subject. "Grandpa," I say. "Where is your family from in Poland?"

"Biala," he answers, "near Krakow."

"What was your family like?" Ever since learning more about Judaism, I have become increasingly interested in my family's ancestry.

"My grandpa was a Torah scribe," he tells me. I'm in shock. Not any man can be a Torah scribe, I have learned; one must have pure thoughts as he writes, or the scroll isn't considered kosher.

"And your father?" I ask. "Was he religious too?"

"In Poland he was, but when he came to America, no."

"What happened?"

"On Yom Kippur, he would see men come to shul and apologize for their sins and then go right back to their old ways the next day. He didn't like the hypocrisy of it." I take in this new information. My paternal great-grandpa shed the tradition I am trying so hard to reclaim. Can I blame him? I too have made the mistake of confusing people with the Torah. More than that, I know how difficult it was to be a religious Jew in America in the early 1900s.

"Did you go to Hebrew school?" I ask my grandpa.

"No," he answers. I can't believe that my great-great-grandpa was a Torah scribe and my grandpa had zero Jewish education.

"I want to take you and your brother Mark out to dinner with Billy tomorrow night," my grandpa tells me, changing the subject. Even though I am not yet strictly kosher, I'm trying not to eat in nonkosher restaurants, especially here in New York, where kosher food is readily available.

That night, behind closed doors, my parents and I discuss the issue — and by discuss, I mean yell at each other.

"You cannot tell Grandpa you keep kosher! Just go wherever he wants to take you and order a salad!" my mom says as loudly as possible without Grandpa overhearing. After Shabbos, I call one of my rabbis from Israel; it turns out salads are actually more of a problem because vegetables need to be checked for bugs. Really, my options are fruit and tea or coffee.

"There are so many kosher restaurants here," I say. "What's the big deal if we go to one of those?"

The next morning, I find grandpa in the living room, reading a book called *Jews and Money*. Classic.

"Grandpa," I say in my sweetest tone, "sorry to interrupt, but would it be okay if we go to a kosher restaurant tonight?"

"I don't eat kosher," my grandpa says.

"That's fine," I say, struggling now for a neutral tone. "I can come, but I just won't be able to eat anything."

Apparently, that's fine with him.

My grandpa, his longtime best friend Billy, my brother, and I are seated at a corner table by the window in a small upscale Italian restaurant. I pretend to peruse the large laminated menu, but I have already decided on a mozzarella-and-tomato salad. After speaking with my rabbi about the various kosher issues, this seems the best option.

When I place my order, Billy says, "That's all you're getting?"

"Yes," I say. "I'm trying to keep kosher…"

Billy turns to my grandpa, who is still looking at his menu. "Henry — I would have gone to a kosher place." My grandpa shakes his head.

I look down. My brother is texting under the table, trying to be discreet. He is oblivious to what's going on.

Once we order, Billy tells me about his kids and grandkids, as usual. He and my grandpa love to brag about his family. How successful and smart they are.

"So, Jenna," my grandpa says with a straight face, "now that you are ultra-Orthodox—"

"Ultra-Orthodox?" I cut him off. I feel my face getting hot. "Grandpa, I am not ultra-Orthodox!"

"Yes, you are. You keep Shabbos and kosher."

"Grandpa," I say, trying to stay calm, "if you want, I can explain to you the difference between the various groups of Orthodox Jews; you will see that I am not ultra-Orthodox…"

"Tell me," he says, "what's with the men who wear goggles in the street?"

"What?" I ask.

"In the paper this morning, I read about ultra-Orthodox men in Brooklyn who wear goggles on the street so that they can't see too far in front of them. They don't want to see anything inappropriate."

I've never heard of such a thing. Even in Israel, I had never seen anything like that.

"Grandpa, that's an extreme custom adopted by a small group of people!" I say.

The meal continues like this, as I pick at my salad and try to debunk the deep-seated prejudice my grandpa has against Orthodox Jews, unsuccessfully.

After two weeks that seemed much longer, Grandpa finally goes back to Florida. We can all breathe again. Still, I can't help but feel that his love for me has diminished somewhat, now that I'm becoming more observant. It is painful; I can only hope that one day he will come around.

CHAPTER 24

Living in Two Worlds

Fall 2011

WHEN I MOVE INTO MY studio apartment in Philadelphia, I finally have my own space. I am not being influenced to be more religious, as I was at Neve; I'm not being pushed to be less religious, as I was at home. I can decide how I want to live.

I have a goal in mind: I want to be fully Torah observant. But I know that I must proceed in steps, or the growth might not be sustainable. And so in those first months of law school, I continue to wear pants and eat vegetarian out.

I'm uncomfortable with the fact that my external appearance doesn't reflect my internal desire. Each morning I get up and stand in my closet thinking, *Skirt...or pants? Skirt? Pants?* Ten minutes go by like this! I am torn. Finally, I decide that Tuesday and Thursday will be pants days, and the rest of the week will be skirts.

It's Shabbos. I'm aware of a religious community nearby, in Lower Merion, about a fifteen-minute drive outside the city, but I don't know anyone to stay with there, so I sit in my apartment with my books and read and sleep. There's an orientation event *motza'ei Shabbos* downtown that I want to go to. Since Shabbos ends so late in the summer, I decide for once to end it on my own time, arbitrarily, so I can attend the event. At 7 p.m., with almost two hours of Shabbos left, I switch on the lights and turn on my phone. I instantly feel a pang of guilt.

I meet up with some friends from high school who are also starting Penn Law, and we drive to the event. The night is ruined from the start; I feel so guilty about breaking Shabbos that I can't relax and enjoy anything. I just want to cry. I promise myself that from now on I will keep Shabbos fully to the best of my ability. Of course, I don't say any of this to my high school friends. In my precarious state, I'm not in a place to explain or defend the spiritual path I'm trying to adhere to.

On Monday I spot a boy in a blue-collared T-shirt and *kippah* climbing the prominent staircase of the law school to our next orientation event. Desperate for an observant friend, I catch up with him and introduce myself. His name is David, and his friend is Naomi. I learn that they both grew up Modern Orthodox.

It turns out that we're all in the same classes. Naomi invites me to her apartment for Shabbos dinner, and I gladly accept.

My first law school class is Civil Procedure with Professor Williams at 9 a.m. Nervous, I try to calm down by listening to a *shiur* on my phone as I head out from my apartment. As I walk up the concrete steps to the grand brick building that houses the law school, I notice the sign beside one of the large wooden doors: First Professor, James Wilson, 1790. James Wilson was one of the first Supreme Court justices appointed by George Washington. The rich American legal history of Philadelphia, of this building, overwhelms me.

I enter our large classroom, with stadium-type seating and wood-paneled walls, and take a seat close to the front, but not too close.

Professor Williams swiftly enters the room in a perfectly tailored suit, carrying a briefcase and a Diet Coke. He looks to be in his early fifties. The small talk in the class immediately ceases. You can hear a pin drop. Everyone sits on the edge of their seats in front of their laptops, hands on the keys, poised to take notes. After he pops open his Diet Coke, he takes a sip and introduces himself. Then he asks everyone to close their laptops. Confused, people grudgingly comply.

"As this is your first day of law school, I want to talk to you about a basic life principle," he begins. Some people write in their notebooks. "No need to take notes. Just listen."

"All of you are A students. You would not have gotten here if you were not. Some of you have never gotten a B in your life. Well, that's about to change. Law school is difficult; you are graded on a curve, and it's impossible for all of you to get A's. More than impossible, it is improbable…" Some students shift uncomfortably in their seats.

"Of course, you will try the best you can. But I'm here to tell you that you need to base your value as a human being on something other than your academic achievements. Grades are not everything in life. The sooner you start this emotional work, the better off you will be. Now that that is settled, I want to talk about some basic principles of civil procedure…"

Students rush to open their laptops again. As Professor Williams speaks, eighty students type away on their keyboards. *Welcome to law school,* I think.

When class is over, I hear some students talking as they pack up. "How dare he tell us not to care about our grades!" one girl mutters.

"I know, like, thanks for telling me I'm not going to get an A," the other girl agrees.

That's not what he said, I want to interject.

Professor Williams has clearly hit a nerve with these girls. But I have found his words refreshing and strangely heartening. In contrast to the scramble around me to form study groups and figure out the best study aids, I take some comfort in the reminder that law school is not everything. I obviously want to do well, but I'm grateful to Neve for instilling this lesson in me earlier that summer. It is my only hope to stay sane in the months that lie ahead.

CHAPTER 25

Make for Yourself a Rabbi

I RECONNECT WITH RABBI LYNN, the MEOR rabbi at Penn, whose Poland trip I was meant to go on at Emory. We have our first meeting at the Penn Hillel, about a ten-minute walk from the law school. We sit at a table in the kosher dining room, which is larger and nicer than I had expected. Unlike at Emory, where Hillel was usually empty, here it's swarming with students. Rabbi Lynn is tall with a neatly trimmed salt-and-pepper beard. He can't be much older than forty.

When I tell Rabbi Lynn I am from Hewlett, he laughs. "The Five Towns. I know it well." It turns out his mom's family is from Long Island, and he spent summers working as a cabana boy at his grandma's beach club in Atlantic Beach. He launches into his best Five Towns housewife impression: "Can you get me a bagel, scooped out, with light tuna on the side..." I laugh, grateful he understands the world I came from.

"I grew up in Palm Beach, Florida," he tells me. "In the days when Jews still weren't allowed in country clubs. My father was a surgeon. I also grew up Reform."

"So what happened?" I ask him.

He laughs. "I can't get into my story, not here, not now. But you're welcome to come hear me tell it the next time I speak to a group of students." I am disappointed but also intrigued.

A few months later, I do hear Rabbi Lynn tell his story. He went to Saint Andrews High School in Boca Raton, which I have passed many a time during my visits to my grandfather. While there, he had to attend church services. When it was time for college, he refused to go to Penn because it was too Jewish (talk about ironic) and opted for Duke instead. He wanted to be a film writer and director and so went on to graduate studies at NYU Film School.

It wasn't until he moved out to Los Angeles that his Jewish journey began. He was writing scripts and developing projects for major studios and living the young Hollywood dream. But the things he most wanted — a spouse, family, wisdom — were nowhere to be found in the business.

The hip part of town, Fairfax/La Brea, shared its streets and alleyways with the religious Jewish community. Rabbi Lynn would often meet fellow creatives in a café in that area on Saturday mornings. He began to take notice of religious people walking past the café, to and from shul, dressed for Shabbos. They piqued his curiosity.

Then finally, one Shabbos, Rabbi Lynn walked into a shul near his local café wearing blue jeans, which clearly pegged him as an outsider. Two *frum* men, writers for a major TV show and themselves *baalei teshuvah*, approached him after services. They schmoozed for a while and then one of the men invited him to his home for Shabbos lunch. At lunch, Rabbi Lynn was struck by the sophistication of his hosts. Not only were they smart and successful, but they were deep and real. So began his Jewish journey of learning Torah, and ultimately going to study in a yeshivah in Israel.

Before we part ways after our first meeting, Rabbi Lynn introduces me to a girl sitting at another table. Laura is also a *baalas teshuvah*. She is a senior in the School of Architecture. We exchange numbers. Rabbi Lynn encourages us both to come to his home in Lower Merion for Shabbos soon.

Although I'm grateful to have some observant friends in law school to spend Shabbos with, I know I also need a rabbi and rebbetzin. A few weeks after our initial meeting, Laura and I take Rabbi Lynn up on his offer to stay at his home in Bala Cynwyd for Shabbos.

The Friday is a typical gray, gloomy Philadelphia day, one where you just want to curl up under the covers. *Is Shabbos still happening?* I wonder, though of course I know it is. Every week, without fail.

We knock on the Lynns' door a few times and a girl about eleven years old answers. She gives us a shy smile and leaves the door open for us to come in. A bunch of kids run around the living room and play. We find Ruthi, Rabbi Lynn's wife, in the kitchen. It smells like chicken soup and fresh challah. Ruthi wears a headscarf and a long black skirt covered in an apron. She welcomes us in as she puts the green beans into the oven.

We try to talk, but the kids keep running in for her attention. Finally, she laughs and rolls her eyes and says in her English accent, "Sara, my oldest daughter, will take you upstairs to your room. I'm going to go up and shower and change, and after we light candles we can schmooze."

When we come back downstairs to light candles in the dining room, order has prevailed over chaos. The long dining room table has been set with an elegant ivory tablecloth, fine china, and wine glasses. Nine-year-old Rosa folds napkins origami-style for each setting.

Ruthi comes downstairs, transformed in a beautiful dress with a shoulder-length brunette wig and makeup. Despite the twins' crying and another child calling her name, she lights her candles with an intense focus. As she covers her eyes and mumbles her prayers, I think I see a few tears roll down her face.

"Good Shabbos," Ruthi says with a smile, giving each of us a hug.

We sit on the soft leather couches by the window. Rabbi Lynn is already at shul. As the kids entertain themselves, more or less, we finally get a chance to introduce ourselves. It turns out that Ruthi did not grow up religious either, although she was raised with more Jewish tradition than Rabbi Lynn. She tells us more about herself: She went to Cambridge University, she has an interest in psychology, and she teaches parenting classes. I am not surprised. I'm already amazed at how she carries any sort of conversation with the commotion around her. She seems to know which child needs attention when and what to say to each one without raising her voice. I would have screamed five times by now!

Before we know it, there is a knock at the door. I hear Rabbi Lynn's voice say, "Good Shabbos!" In the dining room, next to the glow of the candlelight, we sing songs, make Kiddush, and wash our hands for bread. Ruthi's challah is heavenly, with the perfect dense yet fluffy texture and sweet taste. The kids argue over who gets the roasted garlic to spread on it first. After the fish course, we help Ruthi serve the chicken soup. I tell her about my struggles at law school, socially and spiritually. She gets it right away; she went through a similar struggle at Cambridge.

By the time we're on the main course, the kids have drifted off to play or sleep. Laura and I get to ask Rabbi Lynn the deep questions on our minds lately. His thoughtful and compelling answers satisfy both our emotional and intellectual curiosities. I realize that Rabbi Lynn and Ruthi have a strong grasp on not only the Torah, but the world we live in today — we jump from politics to psychology, from philosophy to history. I enjoy their down-to-earth wisdom, their sophisticated perspective on life, and their strong sense of humor. We might be talking about the most serious topic when Ruthi or Rabbi Lynn digresses with a story to illustrate a point that makes us all crack up. I must come back again soon.

CHAPTER 26

Rosh Hashanah Dilemma

THE HIGH HOLY DAYS ARE approaching. My mom calls me. Aunt Lynn is having a Rosh Hashanah dinner at her apartment in New York City, she tells me, and we are all going.

My aunt has moved from the Upper West Side, where there is a large observant Jewish community, to the Upper East Side. I don't know any religious people on the Upper East Side. What my mom doesn't understand is that Rosh Hashanah, and most of the major holidays, are like Shabbos. I can't use electronics or get in a car. Unlike Shabbos, Rosh Hashanah is two days, which means that to go to Aunt Lynn's dinner, I would have to find a place on the Upper East Side to sleep for two nights and kosher meals for the rest of the holiday. I would also need to find a shul I felt comfortable praying in on one of the holiest days of the year. All this for a meal that will not be kosher or focused on the spiritual significance of the holiday in any way. Still, there is something to be said for spending a holiday with your family.

My mom reads the thoughts as they race through my mind. "Jenna. You have to come. Aunt Lynn will tell Grandpa. He's going to know that you've gone off the deep end. That you care more about religion than family. You can't do this." Overwhelmed and confused, I tell her I will call her back.

Why does Torah observance have to be so hard sometimes? I ask myself. I just want to be close to G-d. But the constant separation from friends, family, and classmates is a frustrating burden.

"Jenna, this is a test," my mentor Jackie tells me. "Just like your family challenged you about Shabbos, now they are challenging you about your observance of the holidays. You know that spending Rosh Hashanah on the Upper East Side so you can have dinner at your aunt's is not the right thing for you. Rosh Hashanah is one of the holiest days of the year. I know it's hard now, but you need to be true to yourself. Your parents will understand, eventually. You are not obligated to break Jewish law for them, but you do need to be respectful. Remember, it's okay to have boundaries."

I know Jackie is right. If I want to make Torah observance my own, I need to assert my independence now more than ever. *In the dark, stay true to the light.* I remind myself that I am not doing this to pull away from my family. I'm struggling because I want to be close to them.

I call my mother back and try to convey this, hoping that she'll understand. I tell her that I will spend Rosh Hashanah in Woodmere at Aish Kodesh, so that I can see her and my dad. I will tell my aunt and my grandpa that I'm simply too busy to leave school for the holiday, thereby keeping it simple.

Understandably, my mom is hurt and angry. "Your aunt and your grandpa won't believe you," she warns me.

The next time I speak to my grandpa, he says, "Your aunt tells me you aren't joining your family for the holiday." I'm nervous, but I can't help but laugh to myself. The High Holidays were never a topic of conversation in my family until now!

"No," I say, with a tinge of sadness. "School is really busy and I won't have time to leave for the holidays."

"You know, Jenna," he says, "family is the most important thing in life."

"Of course, Grandpa," I respond. "I know that." With that, we move on to another subject.

The day before I leave for New York, I get my nails done. In the nail place, I overhear a conversation between a young woman and her male friend, who is keeping her company. I gather that both are in the same medical residency program. The guy is not Jewish, but the woman is. He asks her if she's taking off for Rosh Hashanah. She replies that she wishes she could but is saving her day off for Thanksgiving. The conversation deepens into a discussion about their respective religious identities. The woman reveals that even though she is not observant, she is a direct descendent of Rabbi Yisrael Salanter. I can't believe what I'm hearing. I find it sad that this woman, the descendant of such a monumental Jewish leader, would not take off work for Rosh Hashanah.

The first night of the New Year, as my parents drive into the city to my aunt's, I walk with the Moskowitzes to Aish Kodesh. We take our seats as the chazzan begins to sing. Aliza and Illana start praying, but all I can do is look down at the pages of my new machzor (High Holiday prayer book), stained by my fresh tears.

Chapter 27

Shabbos: The Source of Blessing

As I adjust to law school, my life takes on a dual rhythm. During the week I am immersed in law. I come up for air to sleep, eat, exercise, and occasionally meet a friend for a quick dinner. I learn Torah in my "free" time: while I eat, when I walk to and from school, and before I go to bed. But my real spiritual immersion and social time is reserved for Shabbos.

Earlier in the semester, I quickly learned that to keep up with the high demands of law school, I could not keep Shabbos and also go out with law friends. After turning down my high school friends' invitations week after week, they get the point.

MEOR has an apartment on campus, and occasionally the Lynns spend Shabbos at Penn with the students. The first time I go, I realize there's a group of students who, like me, did not grow up religious and are choosing to become more observant. We float our latest questions in observing Jewish law. Do I need to use a separate toothbrush for Shabbos? What is the correct blessing on a strawberry? We discuss deep ideas, like the nature of reality and G-d, which is the reason we care about the blessing on a strawberry in the first place. We laugh about the bizarre challenges we face in school and with our families. I am grateful to have found this spiritual family.

Before law school started, I felt anxious about keeping Shabbos. I didn't know how I was going to take a full twenty-five hours off each week and keep up with my work. After a few months of law school, though, I question how I could live without it. Shabbos is the key to my success and my sanity. It protects me from obsessing about school and careers, as I take time out each week to reconnect with G-d and myself.

Like most type A law students, I'm a hard worker, and the nature of law school is that there is always more work than there is time. If I did not keep Shabbos, there is no way I would give myself the same restorative rest each week; the break I'd likely give myself for a few hours here or there would not be a true rest, but rather a guilt-laden, technology-filled, distracted breather. As finals approach and tension in the law school rises, I see my classmates burning out, while I find that my physical and spiritual recharge each week allows me to work the necessary hard, long hours from Saturday night to Friday afternoon. I don't keep Shabbos for the lifestyle benefits, but I realize how it truly is, as the Torah says, the source of blessing for the week.

Right before finals, I run into one my friends. We talk about — what else — finals. "I don't know how you do it," she says to me.

"Do what?"

"How you stay so calm."

First-semester finals are in fact a big deal. Our entire performance in each class is scored by that one final exam, and these are the grades that future employers will see next summer at on-campus recruitment. Of course I'm nervous like everyone else, and I'm working hard to prepare. But a few thoughts keep me calm. Coming from Penn Law, I know that unless I fail miserably, which is unlikely, I will get a job. Also, as Professor Williams has reminded us, I know that my value is not based solely on my grades. Last, I can go to sleep at night knowing that I am trying my best; the rest is up to G-d.

I feel sorry for my friend who doesn't have this faith. As it turns out, during our first final, she suffers a panic attack and has to leave the exam.

During my second semester I coordinate a lunch-and-learn with Rabbi Lynn in the law school. I shamelessly run around harassing every Jewish law student I can find to come. We bring in trays of free kosher sushi (sponsored by the law school), and Rabbi Lynn, in his usual charismatic fashion, discusses a deep Torah idea and how it relates to us as Jewish law students. A solid group of about fifteen of us enjoy the program, but given how many Jews attend Penn Law, it's a small percentage. Maybe I'm naive, but I'm surprised that even with free food, so many grad students are just not interested or willing to take an hour in their week to talk about some of the deeper questions in life. Despite my friend's panic attack during finals, I cannot coax her to come either.

After one of the lunch-and-learns, Rabbi Lynn asks me how I'm adjusting to Penn. I tell him that even though I am doing well in school and have made friends, deep down I have a nagging feeling that I'm somehow not exactly where I should be. I realize it's partly because I'm having a hard time accepting the fact that I'm in law school and not Neve.

"Jenna," he says, "if you are here, in law school in Philadelphia, then by definition, that's where Hashem wants you to be." I allow his words to sink in. "You're in the best place for you right now," he assures me. "And if law school is where you are, then focus and give it all you've got. G-d willing, you will go back to Israel at the right time. And if you do find some time to go back, I have a former student in mind for you to date. He's there now, studying in yeshivah."

I am still not ready to date for marriage, but the suggestion alone excites me.

Around that time I send my aunt Lynn a birthday card. My dad calls me a few weeks later. Apparently, my aunt took the card to her graphology teacher to analyze my handwriting. My dad tells me what her teacher said: "She lives in two worlds, but they will merge."

CHAPTER 28

Climate Change and Torah

ALTHOUGH I'M GOING THROUGH A deep internal shift in my perspective on the world, I still believe that climate change is a critical issue and that, as caretakers of G-d's earth, we have a responsibility to do what we can to mitigate our impact on the planet. In *Pirkei Avos*, our sages say, "It is not your responsibility to finish the work [of perfecting the world], but you are not free to desist from it either." This is how I feel. I am no longer under the delusion that I will single-handedly save the world (law school grounded me a bit). But I do feel that I must do my part to make the world a safer place for future generations.

As I become more observant, I grapple to reconcile the utopian vision of the Mashiach (Messiah) as laid out in the Torah with the doomsday scenarios I read about in my environmental-studies textbooks. The fact that society and the planet are in a downward spiral of degradation does not contradict the Torah, since the Torah predicts that the "end of days" prior to the coming of the Mashiach will be difficult (also known as the "birth pangs" of the Mashiach). Still, only one of these visions can ultimately manifest. The following question continues to nag at me: Why am I working so hard to prevent the doomsday scenario of mass suicide that environmental scientists predict, when the Torah prophesizes an ultimately bright future where all of humanity will live in peace under the recognition of one G-d?

I present this question to Rabbi Marcus, who is in America visiting colleges again. "Climate change is an issue that needs to be addressed," Rabbi Marcus tells me. "But the Torah tells us that every external issue has a spiritual root or source in reality. So climate change is really just an external manifestation of a deeper spiritual issue."

I am intrigued. "What do you think the spiritual issue is?"

"I think the earth's degradation as manifest in climate change is a reflection of the internal breakdown of humanity. So essentially, you are working on the Band-Aid rather than the root of the problem," he explains.

My initial reaction is anger and confusion. For years I have prided myself on putting my energy into the greatest threat to face humanity in the history of mankind! And now I'm being told that I'm approaching the issue from only the most superficial level?

I didn't fully agree with Rabbi Marcus then. But his answer initiates a dialogue between myself, climate science, the Torah, and several rabbis throughout my time at Penn, all of whom give varying responses to my question. I keep coming back to Rabbi Marcus's answer, though, as it makes the most sense to me.

It would be one thing if I enjoyed law, but in the same way that I view Jewish law as a means to connect to G-d, I view American law as a necessary means to effect climate-change policy. And as graduate school goes on, I feel more and more that my work on climate change is not as meaningful as I'd thought it to be. I need to feel that my work is deeply, not superficially, significant. It's an unsettling realization as I expend increasing time and energy toward my graduate degree.

CHAPTER 29

Back to the Shtetl

IN THE WINTER BREAK OF my second year of law school, I finally go on the Poland trip I have been destined to take since my senior year at Emory — but really, it's a trip I've been destined to go on my whole life. Ever since I was a young child, I've had an obsessive fascination with the Holocaust. I read every book I could get my hands on as I tried to understand how human beings could carry out such a massive atrocity and how the world could silently stand by and allow it to happen. I also felt a strong connection, a longing even, for the traditional European shtetl life that my ancestors ran away from.

On a cloudy December day, my group and I walk through the empty Madjanek concentration camp, between rows of dark-wood barracks and an abandoned watchtower. We are mostly quiet and contemplative, though I hear a few soft-spoken conversations around me. Mostly I hear our boots crunching on the snow. I pull my thick hood over my head to avoid the frigid air on my face. Despite wearing three to four layers of warm clothing, I'm embarrassed to admit I am cold. Two friends walk beside me, wrapped inside an Israeli flag.

There is a long stretch in front of us, and we continue to walk down it. Outside the camp fence are condominiums. How the Poles who live in them can bear the view of a former death camp every day is beyond me.

Eventually we turn the corner and walk toward a small building a bit removed from the camp. No one tells us where we are going, and I don't want to admit it to myself when I realize what it is. I want to turn around, but feel it my duty to go inside. We walk down the same path that thousands of Jews had to walk down before us, knowing full well that they were meeting their deaths. What were they thinking about? How did they feel? How many attempted to run away at this moment to meet their death as a free person?

Slowly we enter the former gas chamber, an empty room with bare gray walls. It is dark and dank; the only light streams in from the open door. The group spreads out into a circle, facing my rabbi. I place a few fingers on the cold, damp walls and shudder, as I picture the people who touched this wall before me. I see their scratch marks on the walls. I imagine thin, naked bodies slumped over each other in a pile on the floor. I feel like I am going to vomit and faint.

Although I can't bear to touch it, I hold on to the wall as lightly as possible to remain conscious. But as my rabbi speaks I can hardly focus. I want to run out of here so badly. I am shaking and dizzy. I look around at the group — solemn faces dressed in heavy coats and hats and boots. I wonder what each person thinks when my rabbi insists, "You have to have a heart of stone not to cry in a place like this." White air streams from their mouths when they exhale. Dead silence, tears flowing, scared eyes. We are in the trenches of the history of our people.

I glance back at my rabbi every now and then. His scruffy beard is turning gray. He has led almost a dozen trips to Poland. I don't understand how he can descend into such darkness each year and emerge positive and inspired from the trip.

I reflect on the years I spent studying the Holocaust through memoirs, culminating in a Holocaust Memoir course at Emory with the renowned Holocaust historian Deborah Lipstadt. As strange as it sounds, those memoirs were comforting, because they provided a link to my people and my past, to many unknown ancestors. But there is nothing comforting about the death trap I stand in now. I can't believe that this was what all of those memoirs and seminar discussions come down to: this small, stark room.

I fight the urge to escape several times, until finally my rabbi leads us all in the Shema, the last words on so many Jewish lips. The group moves on to the crematorium in the next chamber. When I catch sight of a row of black metal ovens, I turn around and walk out. I find some sort of rock to sit on and sob loudly.

I cry for my grandma and great-grandpa, two American Jews who made a freewill decision to do to their bodies what the Nazis did to so many Jews against their will. I cry for my grandpa, who also wants to be cremated when the time comes, despite my attempts to dissuade him otherwise. I cry for the Jews who had to live in these camps and the immense suffering they endured. But most of all I cry for G-d, that He had to allow this to happen to His people, for whatever reason. I don't understand, and I cry for Him.

I am in such a pit of darkness that I ask myself how I can go on and live a normal life after this. But then I remember words from the Torah: *"I have placed before you life and death: Choose life."* I have to choose life for G-d and for the murdered. As we get back onto the warm bus, those words are my only consolation.

CHAPTER 30

Human Survival, Jewish Survival

"So," my professor declares, closing his ten-minute rant, "through the global climate-change crisis, we are committing mass suicide as a species and are thus perpetrating a global holocaust."

My hand shoots up. I look at the ten other students sitting around the small conference table in the intimate rare-book library room at Penn Law. How are they silent? Most of them aren't listening; they doodle in their notebooks, since laptops aren't allowed in this class.

"Excuse me," I say. "I have to admit, I take personal offense at the use of the word 'holocaust' in this context. This is not a genocide situation where a group of people are being targeted for murder. We are altering our natural environment in a way that may not be sustainable for future generations. The two are very different things." The professor and I go back and forth for a while. I can't believe he can even argue this point.

Truthfully, he is not a real professor but a law librarian, who is using this class to test out his "Law and Human Survival" book manuscript.

In another chapter of his book, he suggests that it is morally irresponsible to have children, due to the global population crisis. Again, my class remains mostly passive, but I'm outraged. If no one has children, then we will surely commit mass suicide as a species! Surely that is not morally responsible. Besides, the Torah commands us to be fruitful and multiply. I decide to write my final paper on sustainability from a Torah perspective.

I find a significant number of Torah sources that support caring for the earth. The Torah has mitzvot that include preventing waste, compassion to animals, and sustainable land use. On a deeper level, the Torah describes nature as a continuous miracle from G-d that because of its regularity seems natural. Thus, Torah-observant Jews believe that since the physical world is an expression of the spiritual world, keeping all the mitzvot is central to maintaining a stable external world.

So if a Jew did not have a child for the sake of keeping the global population down, the spiritual impact of all the mitzvot that one child would have done could potentially have a greater impact on preventing environmental destruction than one less child in the world could on a more external, natural level.

The paper also forces me to finally confront the apparent contradiction between the doomsday scenario of environmental scientists and the Torah vision of a spiritual utopia when Mashiach comes. I learn that the two paths are not necessarily contradictory, because Torah sources describe that Mashiach can come in one of two ways: through either the elevation or the degradation of society. If the Jewish people, and through their example all of humanity, reach their spiritual potential, we can earn the arrival of Mashiach, who will come on *kanfei nesharim*, "eagle's wings." The second scenario is that the Jewish people, and consequently the rest of humanity, will have sunk to the lowest possible level before destruction, necessitating the arrival Mashiach, who it is said will come on a donkey. So for Torah-observant Jews, the idea is to do as many mitzvot as possible and work to enhance society, which creates *tikkun olam* (repair of the world) so that we can bring

Mashiach to us in the ideal way. One can and should still recycle and conserve electricity, but to address the problem on an internal, spiritual level, I realize, mitzvot are needed.

CHAPTER 31

My First Shidduch Date

Summer 2013

I HAVE A FEW PRECIOUS weeks of freedom before my summer job begins, so I plan a three-week trip to Israel. Rabbi Lynn decides that the time is ripe for me to meet Ben,* his former student who is now in yeshivah, the one whom he thinks could be my husband.

I am in CVS, buying toiletries, when Rabbi Lynn calls me. "Jenna, I know I hyped up this *shidduch* match between you and Ben, but I think it's best if you both go into this with low expectations, to ease the pressure." He's right; there is a lot of pressure. After dating in the secular world, where one can date someone for years before even discussing marriage, I find the marriage-minded approach refreshing and efficient. At the same time, each date carries significantly more weight.

"Remember," Rabbi Lynn says, "the first few dates are just to see if you guys like spending time with each other. Don't ask yourself: *Can I see myself marrying this person? That comes a bit later, around date five or six.*" *Date five or six?!* "For now, ask yourself: *Do I like hanging out with this person?*"

Still, a while later as I get dressed for our first date in my room at Neve, where I'm learning on this trip, I feel like I am going to vomit. I'm all too aware of the *shidduch* crisis in the religious world.

---

* Name has been changed to protect privacy.

I am twenty-four, which is approaching "old maid" in that world, but not yet. Especially not in circles of *baalei teshuvah*, who tend to marry older. I'm looking for someone who ideally became religious later on in life like me. On top of that, I need someone grounded who has a profession.

"You're being too narrow-minded. The pool of people you're dating in is too small," my mom told me before I left for the trip. "You need to widen your options. It's okay if the guy is not as Orthodox as you are."

Maybe she's right, I found myself thinking. Yet I hadn't even begun religious dating, and I was already supposed to compromise on the single most important thing to me, my husband's commitment to Torah and Hashem? The very thing that I'd fought so hard to obtain for myself? I was unable to do that, not at that point.

I finally responded, "Mom, if Hashem created me, He created someone who will be the right fit for me."

I need to believe this is true.

Ben and I meet at a café in downtown Jerusalem. He is nice-looking and clean-shaven, with black hair and a pale complexion. He wears a black suit and a black velvet *kippah.* The waitress shows us to our reserved table in the corner, with a small candle in the middle. We begin to talk about our journeys to Judaism, because that is obviously the area of most common ground.

When I started law school, I became *shomer negia* (literally, "guard the touch"). I had learned that the idea behind it is to preserve the intimacy of touch for marriage. Yet I soon realized that refraining from touch was only part of the picture. I also became sensitive to what I shared with men. I didn't want a man I wasn't even dating to be privy to my feelings and thoughts. Real modesty, I learned, is knowing what to share, and with whom.

Now, sitting across the table from Ben, I'm finally free to open up. Yet I am scared and feeling incredibly vulnerable. There is something so raw about baring your soul to another human being who is judging you on the deepest level, all the while wondering to yourself if this is someone you want to spend the rest of your life with.

We go on a couple of pleasant dates. Despite my nervousness, our conversation flows nicely, and I begin to get excited that he could be the one. We talk about our families, school, career aspirations, what we love about Torah. After each date, I replay our conversations in my head. *Why did I say that?* I ask myself. *I should have said this.* And then I replay the scene with my chosen script. I constantly check my phone between classes at Neve as I wait for Rabbi Lynn to call me, to let me know if Ben wants to see me again. In other words, I drive myself crazy.

After our third date, I call Rabbi Lynn right away to say that I would like to go out again. After all, the conversation was nice and we come from similar backgrounds and have a similar vision for what type of home we'd like to have — and Rabbi Lynn thinks this could be my husband!

However, Rabbi Lynn meets my excitement with hesitation. "Ben wants to go out again too," he says, "but he feels like there is a chemistry that might be missing. Don't be so serious, try to relax."

My face turns hot. I can't believe my rabbi just told me to relax! I become insecure, knowing now that Ben doesn't like me as much as I like him. The next date is more awkward because I am self-conscious and trying to force myself to relax. It is not natural, and I feel it.

Still, Ben is "willing to give it another try," and we go bowling so we can have a more "laid-back" date. Really, what I need is a drink to loosen up, but I do the best I can to chill. Even though Rabbi Lynn has warned me not to, I can't help but hear his words, which I deeply respect — *"I think this could be your husband"* — and it taints my view of the situation. I realize I am trying to win Ben.

Rabbi Lynn calls me a day later. "Ben thinks you are a great girl, but you're just not his wife."

Ouch.

"I'll be okay," I tell him, tears welling in my eyes. I've never felt so judged — and rejected — in my life. I am humiliated. Just like that, I will never speak to Ben again.

A few days later, a friend refers me to a rabbi in the Old City of Jerusalem who can tell you about your essence and your life purpose based on your Hebrew name and your birthday.

When I knock on the door of the rabbi's modest home, a man with a colorful knitted *kippah*, tan skin, and a long white beard greets me with a warm smile. He motions for me to follow him to the long wooden dining room table. I can hear his wife in the kitchen.

After I tell him my Hebrew name, Miriam, and my Hebrew birthday, 21 Cheshvan, the rabbi spends a few minutes reading two worn-out books.

He goes to the kitchen and brings back two cups of water, one cup smaller than the other. "See these cups?" he asks me. "They are both filled with the same amount of water. But one cup is only half-filled, while the other is filled."

I nod my head, unsure of where he is going with this.

"You are capable of many things," he tells me. "Just because you can do something that is fulfilling for others does not mean it is going to 'fill your cup,' so to speak."

I tell him about my path in law. How all my peers are so content just to be at Penn Law and to get a firm offer, but I am longing for more. I tell him about my desire to spend more time learning in Israel.

"The only thing worse than having no intuition is not following your intuition," he warns me. "Do not listen to what others say you need to be successful. You don't want to drag your feet through life;

you want to live a life of vitality." I take in his words for a moment.

"Bitterness is a big theme for you, since the root of Miriam, *mar*, means 'bitter' in Hebrew. Also, the month of Cheshvan in which you were born is referred to as Marcheshvan, the bitter month, because we do not celebrate any holidays during this month. You were born on the twenty-first. The number twenty-one is the numerical equivalent of one of G-d's Names, which means 'I will be what I am.' Hashem is the same G-d, regardless of whether we see His manifestation as one of love or punishment.

"Part of your purpose is to know that things are good now, not once you have clarity, but right now, even when you feel in the dark, because G-d is ultimately good. Do not let yourself fall into bitterness. Through your *emunah*, your faith, you can raise yourself up and the others around you."

Know that it is good now, I repeat to myself. The timeliness of this message hits me, and I am filled with emotion. I know the rabbi's words are true. That I need to have faith that the right person is out there for me, and at the right time I will meet him. But after what happened with Ben, my heart can't embrace this reality. Not yet. I understand why the Torah teaches that the farthest distance in the world is between one's head and one's heart.

CHAPTER 32

Summer at the Firm

I REALLY WANT TO DO public-interest law after graduation. I've worked at a nonprofit law firm and the Environmental Protection Agency, but jobs at these places are almost impossible to get right out of law school. Penn Law is a feeder school for large, private law firms. These jobs pay well, but they demand almost all your time and energy.

I go on some halfhearted interviews for private firm jobs. As I wait to begin my second-round interview at a large New York City firm, I use the bathroom and notice showers there. Showers. Obviously, people spend so much time at the office that showers are required. Or maybe the showers are meant to encourage people to spend more time at the office. Either way, I find it disturbing.

In the end, I accept an offer from an environmental-law firm, one that seems more "lifestyle friendly," as they call it. One with no showers.

This summer is a trial. If I perform well and the firm thinks I'm a good fit, I'll get an offer after graduation. Despite my conflicted feelings, I'm determined to dedicate myself to the job so that I at least have the option of an offer. And although the firm is generally a pleasant place to work, it is not always easy. When I'm asked to write a memo that essentially twists the law so that our client can claim it is polluting legally, I hold my tongue and smile. When one of the named partners, Mr. Kraus,* sits behind his large mahogany desk and insults my diligence and intelligence, I again hold my tongue and smile.

Sometimes the partners take the summer associates out to lunch. During these two-hour affairs I try to engage, although I often sit there picking at my homemade kosher meal, wondering if the conversation will ever turn to anything more meaningful than TV, sports, or drinking.

Even a "lifestyle friendly" firm job is extremely demanding, I realize. The partners have families, but it is obvious that most of their time, and the best part of themselves, goes to their work. Only a few of the lawyers seem genuinely happy. The rest are stressed and overworked. No wonder their hobbies are mind-numbing.

One afternoon I go across the street to eat my sandwich. Just as I start to say the after blessing, I look up. Mr. Kraus is standing there, with his round thin-rimmed glasses and balding head. He tries to initiate conversation. *Oh, G-d.* I can't answer until I've finished the blessing, which takes me about two minutes. I feel my face get hot. I hold up a finger: "One minute." He nods and proceeds to check emails on his phone. I say the blessing with as much concentration as I can, telling myself that this job and my life are in G-d's hands, not Mr. Kraus's. When I look up, he is gone. I've taken too long.

When I return to my desk, I attempt to push through the afternoon slump. Amid the stacks of cases I need to read, the incessant dinging of my email on my computer, and the throat clearing of the associate at the next desk, I look up and think, *Is this going to be my life?*

---

* Name has been changed to protect privacy.

CHAPTER 33

Permission to Be Me

Fall 2013

BACK AT NEVE I HAD pledged to myself to return to Israel after graduating law school. Now, on the verge of graduation, this seems like a pipe dream. I feel immense pressure to get a legal job after the education my family financed. Still, the idea of Israel keeps resurfacing.

Most of my friends have obtained their coveted firm offers. I apply to public-interest fellowships and clerkships. When I prepare for the interviews, I draft answers to questions like Why do you want to work here? and How does this job fit into your overall career goals? I'm forced to confront the fact that as hard as I try to convince myself and my hypothetical employers otherwise, I am not passionate about these jobs. I don't know what my ultimate career goal is anymore.

I decide to meet with the public-interest career counselor at the law school. As I sit in the big leather chair opposite her, I grow more and more frustrated. None of the jobs she is presenting feel like a good fit for me, but I can't fully articulate why. She doesn't know much about me, either. Finally, she looks at me, and in what might be one of the most revealing moments of my life, she says, "When I have these sorts of conversations with students, it's usually because they're too scared to say what they really want: either they don't want to practice law and want to be a businessman, or they want to be a politician, or they want to be a writer. Jenna, it sounds like you just want to be a writer."

And there it is. I try to hold back the tears. A woman who hardly knows me is telling me something that I can't even admit to myself. I can't admit it partly because I feel guilty betraying the climate-change cause. But let's be honest: What I really feel guilty about is betraying my mother. I am terrified. Yes, a Jewish mother can be scarier than a global threat to humanity.

My mother. The woman counting on me to live out her own unfulfilled dream to become a successful professional. The pressure cannot be understated. We have an innate desire to be loved and accepted by our parents. I am also scared of my grandpa. He expects me to be a successful lawyer and has invested in me, in my education, for this purpose. I can't tell him that now I'm going to be a writer!

I joke to people that law school is killing my soul, but I'm partly serious. I've had rare moments of clarity where my soul has cried out, *Go back to Israel,* or *Become a writer,* or *Law is not for me.* These cries have been silenced by the tasks at hand or sheer exhaustion. But now graduation is approaching and I must decide: Am I going to live my life or someone else's?

One Friday afternoon in October as I drive to the Lynns' to stay with them for Shabbos, I get a call from my cousin. She is a judge and wants to help me get an environmental-law job at the district attorney's office in Queens. As she rattles off what I need to do to apply, my throat becomes hoarse and I fight a rising anxiety. *No, no, no!* is all I can think. Finally I manage to respond, "Thank you. I'm still trying to figure out what I'm doing next year. I may want to go to Israel — "

"Go to Israel?" she exclaims, cutting me off. "How are you going to get a job when you get back? What about — ?"

She introduces my close friends, Fear and Doubt. Little does she know I am with them each day. Every morning I battle with them when I pray to G-d so fervently, begging, *Please, give me clarity. Guide me as to what I should do next year.* When yet another friend tells me her plans after graduation, and I begin to panic. Or when I'm at the gym and my thoughts hop on the same mental treadmill. I try to spend more time with my friends Faith and Trust. I always feel calmer and happier with them. But they tend to be elusive, especially with Fear and Doubt hanging around all the time.

There is a quote on my fridge that gives me comfort: "Do not tell Hashem how big your problems are; tell your problems how big Hashem is." I tell myself that G-d can do anything. Anything! He can get me the right job. And more than that, He is guiding me, and I am exactly where I need to be right now. Take that, Fear and Doubt.

Other times I crumble. Like when I am on the phone with my cousin, who makes me feel insane for even mentioning Israel.

I almost can't believe it when I arrive at the Lynns' and realize what this week's parshah, Torah portion, is: *Lech Lecha*. It is what G-d told Abraham: *"Go for yourself*, from your land, from your birthplace, and from your father's house, to the land which I will show you."

To me the message could not be more clear or timely: Return to Israel. Return to the person you are meant to be.

I can't ignore these messages anymore. With a mix of fear and exhilaration, I begin to write for ten minutes each day. A quiet reclamation of myself. Before long, I compose a letter to my family:

> *My dear parents,*
> *I am writing this letter so you may understand where I'm coming from. I hope you can.*

Our society generally teaches that money and success equal happiness. It is true that self-actualization does increase happiness, but for some, self-actualization may not lead to the money they want, and so they end up selling out. I am surrounded by such people at law school, clearly intelligent, gifted people who aren't passionate about being lawyers or truly happy at all, but just going through the motions that will set them on a financially secure track. They seem to march through life like robots, silently accepting the confines of society. I find it oppressive. The saddest thing of all is that most of them haven't begun to answer questions like "Why am I here?" or "What is most important in life?" And it's these questions that are at the heart of a Torah lifestyle.

At Neve, the teachers and students joke that seminary is the university of life. When you learn Torah, you learn about every facet of reality, and thus you better understand yourself, your place in the world, and how to live a life with values and meaning. I have been learning Torah as a side job during my time in law school. But it is too important to constantly be put on the backburner… There are hundreds of other law students who can take any of the jobs I'm applying to, but no one else can be a mother to my future children. I want to have the spiritual strength to build a home with children who are inspired to be the best they can be and carry on the tradition that our people have had for thousands of years.

My last point is difficult to explain, but I feel, deep down, that I am meant to spend time in Israel, that it is part of fulfilling my life's purpose… I know there are practical considerations. Money is important, as is job security. But I wanted to write to remind you of the other considerations in the picture.

To repeat a famous quote: I don't just want to go through life, I want to grow through life. Please give me your blessing to undertake the journey I need to go on to become the person Hashem created me to be.

I love you,
Jenna

Although my parents understand my position, the bottom line is that they do not want me to go to Israel, and I don't want to go without their blessing. I pray that Hashem intervenes.

CHAPTER 34

The Sea Splits

I KNOW ON THE DARK-WOOD door of Professor Ziegler's makeshift office — makeshift because she is a visiting law professor from Israel, teaching a onetime course on the legal aspects of the Israeli and Palestinian conflict.

"Come in!" she says in a cheerful voice with a thick Israeli accent. I find her sitting at a small, round table. Professor Ziegler is middle-aged, with short brown hair that she covers with a hat and a slim pencil skirt that reaches her knees. She is Modern Orthodox and does not hold classes on the Jewish holidays. She takes a liking to me and my friend Naomi, who are the only other observant Jews in the class.

I am hoping that Professor Ziegler might help me get to Israel somehow.

"Jenna, I just want to say how impressed I am with how you're doing in the class. You have a strong grasp of the material, and your participation is excellent," she tells me matter-of-factly. I thank her. I begin to explain how I want to spend time in Israel next year, ideally studying in seminary but also perhaps working in law.

"Have you thought about clerking in the Supreme Court of Israel as a foreign clerk?" she asks.

"My Hebrew isn't good enough," I reply.

"You don't need to know Hebrew," she assures me. "All the justices and their Israeli clerks speak English. Your job as a foreign clerk is to research American, European, and international law for the justices to assist them in their cases."

"That sounds great," I say. I wonder if I will be able to work in the court and also study in the seminary, or if it's a full-time position.

"If you decide to apply, I'm happy to write you a letter of recommendation," she tells me.

It turns out that the foreign clerk position at the Supreme Court of Israel is full-time, but not necessarily for the whole year. I apply to clerk for the fall term so that I can work in the court half the year and study in seminary the other half. After I submit the application, I hear nothing for almost a month. Then I get an email from the chambers of one of the female justices, scheduling me for an interview the following week.

I interview with two of the justice's Israeli clerks. They tell me that I will probably hear back in about two weeks. I wait anxiously and pray each day. *Please, G-d, let me get this job if it will be good for me.*

Less than a week later, I wake up on the morning of my birthday, November 18. After I say *Modei Ani*, I scroll through my email on my phone, and there it is: a message from Tal, the clerk I interviewed with. I see the first words of the email before even opening it: "I am pleased to inform you…"

I jump out of bed, shaking with joy. I call my parents. They are overjoyed about my acceptance of the job and suddenly supportive of my trip to Israel. Just like that. I feel as if G-d has split the sea for me: I can now go to Israel and learn Torah with the support of my parents! I didn't know if it was possible. I just hoped and prayed, and Hashem showed me the way. I have never felt so grateful.

CHAPTER 35

Superwoman

Spring 2014

IN MY LAST SEMESTER OF graduate school, I'm working 24/6 to finish my master's thesis on climate change and sea-level rise when I get an email that I have been chosen to receive the Dean's Scholars Award on behalf of the College of Liberal and Professional Studies master's programs at Penn. This is apparently a high honor.

I'm glad I can give my parents *nachas*. But more than that, I get *nachas* from myself. I'm proud that during my time at Penn I did not compromise my values, and despite keeping Shabbos (really, *because of* keeping Shabbos), I was able to excel academically. Though I don't say it out loud, I am glad my parents and the Penn community see this too.

We sit at our assigned table in the reception room at the post-award dinner. There are two other award recipients at our table with their families. Each table also has a distinguished alumna or alumnus present. Our alumna, dressed in a classic black dress and pearls, sits to my right. As the waiters serve the salad, we begin talking. She is a high-powered lawyer in New York City. She lives on the Upper East Side and has one child. Her husband is also a lawyer.

The waiter serves my kosher salad in a plastic tray. She glances over from her iPhone to see what I'm eating and then gets right back to her email, her eyebrows wrinkled. When she does put her phone down, we talk more about her work. Her tone is very matter-of-fact; there is no passion.

I look at my parents, sitting to my other side. Their eyes glisten as they gaze at me expectantly. They want to join the conversation but are unsure of themselves.

An administrator from the College of Liberal and Professional Studies stops by our table. Apparently, she is the one who identified me for this award. My parents shake her hand and thank her profusely for choosing me for this honor.

"It wasn't a hard decision," she tells them. "When I saw Jenna's resume, I thought to myself, 'This girl is Superwoman!'"

"She is Superwoman!" my mom agrees, beaming.

I smile and take in her words. Lately, I've been spending more and more time with the Lynns. I observe how Ruthi, despite her Cambridge degree, chose to focus on raising children. She responds with as much patience as she can while her children cry, scream, beg, or simply call for her attention over and over. Despite the tumultuous activity of eight kids in the house, she makes herself available to countless students and community members who seek her wisdom and guidance. And she cooks for at least a dozen people each Shabbos.

I think about my parents, who have given my brother and me everything so that we could achieve what they could not. Their private acts do not get the same recognition as my public achievements, but to my mind they are far greater. To refine your character and constantly give of yourself to other people, especially those closest to you, is much harder than anything I have ever done. Yes, I did go to graduate school to work on a public policy issue, which is noble. But if I'm being honest, I have also toiled away over the past seven years in college and graduate school to prove to everyone — and myself — that I am worthy.

Now my worthiness has received public acknowledgement. I

did it. I am doing it. Doing what? I'm on track to be like the woman to my right, but I really want to be like Ruthi, like my parents. I wonder if I won the race only to find out I was running the wrong race the whole time. It is faintly exhausting.

CHAPTER 36

"Yah Not Goin'"

Summer 2014

I WALK THROUGH THE CEMETERY, past the lines of gravestones engraved with Hebrew writing and down the narrow path leading to the Ohel, the resting place of the Lubavitcher Rebbe. Although I am not Chabad myself, I feel pulled to daven (pray) in this place, in the merit of this tzaddik. The last few weeks have been growing more and more intense.

I returned to New York after graduation to study for the bar exam. After weeks of studying, I still don't feel ready. Such is the cruelty that is the bar exam; it is impossible to cover all of the testable material.

There is another tension, though. Earlier in the summer, three young Jewish yeshivah students were kidnapped in Israel by Hamas terrorists. The entire Jewish world mobilized to pray for "our boys," who were thought to be lost. Weeks later, I saw the update on my phone: The boys had been found murdered. I began to sob. I didn't even know these boys, yet they were family. This incident sparked a war between Israel and Gaza. Every day now, rockets rain down on Israel as Israelis run into bomb shelters for cover.

I am scheduled to go to Israel two weeks after the bar exam. As the war intensifies, the tension in my house rises. My mom hovers over me, anxious to say what is on her mind, but holding back for fear of distracting me from my studying.

Finally, one night as I review some practice questions at the kitchen table before dinner, she stands over me and says, in her native Brooklyn accent, "Yah not goin."

I look up. "What?"

"Yah not goin' to Israel," she repeats.

We go back and forth. I assure her that we will assess the rapidly changing situation closer to my departure date. I promise her that if it's too dangerous, I won't go. But I will make this decision based on speaking to people who actually live in Israel, as opposed to the media reports, where my well-meaning mother gets her information. Understandably, she doesn't like my answer.

The Torah says that the Land of Israel is acquired only through suffering. This explains why every time I attempt a trip to Israel it is a struggle. I am afraid I don't have much more energy to fight.

I decide to go to the holiest place I know that is closest to my parents' home: the Ohel. I had learned that if a truly holy person, a tzaddik, petitions to G-d on your behalf, then G-d will answer you because He does not want to say no to a tzaddik. I need all the help I can get.

Although my dad thinks I'm crazy, he agrees to drive. As we pull up to the entrance, a few chassidim walk by with their long beards, black hats, and black silk coats.

"Don't be nervous, Dad," I tell him.

"I'm just scared that this is where you feel comfortable!" he says. We both laugh for a moment. He insists on waiting for me in the car.

I walk into the Ohel, into a small room with bare wooden shelves covered in tea lights and prayer books. I light a candle and then enter the women's side. There are only a few people here tonight, but the silence is heavy as each person stands over the *kever*, pouring his heart out.

I take out my siddur. My stomach is in knots. I am scared that I may not pass the bar. After weeks and weeks of grueling studying, I'm scared that I may have to endure this torture all over again for something I no longer really want. I'm scared to move to Israel, a war zone, as my mom calls it. Yet the idea of not going is even scarier. Will I get my parents' blessing in the end? I am afraid of the unknown. What is going to be with me? When will I meet the right guy? What type of job will I get after taking a year off in Israel?

These are the thoughts that pour out of my heart that summer night at the Ohel, where all I can hear are crickets and my own silent pleas. I pray for myself, for my friends, for my family, for the Jewish people, for Israel.

After I finish praying, I look up, and in front of me, on the concrete ledge surrounding the *kever*, I notice a small white magnet that reads, Relax…smile. Only Hashem is in control. Ein od milvado. I immediately relax and smile. It is clear that G-d has heard me and answered with the reassurance that He controls everything and wants what is ultimately good, always.

Fall 2014

After I took the bar, my friends in Jerusalem reassured me that it was safe enough to come. With these assurances, I told my parents that I was going, and I would be safe. After weeks of fighting, they relented.

I am in the *sherut*, on the way from Ben Gurion airport to my apartment. I will be living in Nachlaot, near the Machaneh Yehuda *shuk* (market), in the heart of downtown Jerusalem. I have always wanted to live in Nachlaot, with its artists, vegans, and religious hippies. Through *hashgachah pratis*, a friend from Penn has introduced me to Shayna, an American living in Nachlaot who has been looking for a roommate. I am thrilled.

I give the *sherut* driver my address. Nachlaot is a labyrinth of winding, narrow streets that a *sherut* cannot drive down. By the time we figure out the best drop-off point, the driver is yelling at me for making him go ten minutes out of his way. He continues to berate me as he unloads my big black overweight suitcases and chucks them onto the busy street corner off Agripas Street, the main thoroughfare. He drives away and there I am, standing with a pile of luggage amid honking horns, crowds of people streaming past me, and store merchants shouting at each other in Hebrew. Welcome to Israel.

A few nights after I arrive, my new roommate Shayna invites me to a Torah class at a nearby rebbetzin's home. I recognize the rebbetzin's name; she's supposed to be amazing.

We walk past the *shuk* toward Geula, the insular, ultra-Orthodox enclave where she lives. In just a few blocks, the colorful, diverse group of tourists and secular and religious Israelis and Arabs gives way to chassidim dressed in black and white. I'm careful not to wear anything too colorful. My long black maxi skirt and gray sweater are safe choices.

The rebbetzin's walls are lined with bookshelves of *sefarim* from top to bottom. Though the rebbetzin herself is American, there are no English books in sight. We find seats in the crowded room. Some young women sit on the floor.

The rebbetzin is a Breslov chassid. Her outfit is simple, and she doesn't wear any makeup, but she radiates warmth. From the moment the rebbetzin opens her mouth to teach, I am entranced. She discusses how we should handle difficult times in spiritual growth. How we need to hold on to whatever level we are on and encourage ourselves, rather than beat ourselves up if we are having a hard time. To feel bad for ourselves is a luxury we can't afford, she says. She quotes a variety of classic Torah sources off the top of her head and intersperses her teachings with chassidic stories. I drink in every word. For the entire hour, my pen doesn't leave the pages of my notebook.

"This is why I've come to Israel," I hear myself say. Only in Israel can one find so many people with "Torah glasses" on, people who really understand the purpose of life and actually live that reality. I've come here to absorb wisdom from such people, people like the rebbetzin.

CHAPTER 37

Life at the Court

"I DIDN'T THINK YOU WOULD come," my justice says in her thick Israeli accent. She sits behind a large dark-wood desk, tall shelves of legal books behind her. "Do you have family in Israel?"

"No. But I've spent some time learning here, so I'm close to a few families and I have friends here," I explain.

"Where did you learn?" When I answer Neve, she looks at me quizzically. I add that it's a seminary, in Har Nof. She nods. Most of the people at the court are *chiloni*, or secular Israelis, with the exception of a few male justices. I haven't seen a woman in a skirt yet.

She gets to the point. "We are working on a case where the main issue is whether terrorists in prison should have the right to higher education." I begin to take notes on my legal pad. "I need you to look at the constitutionality of this issue in America law, but also European law and international law."

I leave the justice's chambers and enter the bright, long hallway, which has large glass windows on one side and Jerusalem stone on the other. The architecture of the court itself, which combines both modern and ancient elements, reflects an underlying tension I can sense already: Is Israel a Jewish state or a democratic state? Can it be both? I can't help but laugh that Israel concerns itself with the educational rights of terrorists whose purpose is to see the country destroyed.

I head back to my desk in a corner of the law library, where I

work side by side with the other justices' foreign clerks. We are
a diverse group of Americans, Canadians, and Europeans, repre-
senting the many jurisdictions we research. Yet we're all recent
law grads who've chosen to work in Israel. We are mostly, but not
exclusively, Jewish. None of the other female clerks are religious,
but a few of the male clerks are Modern Orthodox.

One afternoon the Modern Orthodox guys invite me to join
them in *minchah*, the afternoon service. We head to the elevator
and descend into the belly of the court and through a labyrinth of
hallways and stairs, until we reach an unfinished meeting room in
the basement with scattered chairs and file boxes.

There is no *mechitzah*, or wall divider, as there are no women
who typically pray in the court. The men trickle in, a mix of Israeli
administrative staff and janitors, American foreign clerks, and two
male justices. I end up praying behind a projector screen, feeling
silly and out of place.

The next week, I debate whether to pray with the men again. I
don't feel so comfortable there as the only woman. When I reluctantly return downstairs with the men to pray, I notice a wooden
mechitzah positioned in the middle of the room. It turns out that
Ariel, the foreign clerk, bought it, thinking it improper that the
court didn't have one to accommodate the women — or in this
case, a woman. Now I feel obligated to pray with the men. And
this is how I find myself the only woman praying daily with the
minyan in the Supreme Court of Israel.

One day, two of the other female clerks and I go across the street
to Cinema City for lunch. The two other clerks, Michelle and
Karen, often ask me questions about religious dating and other
Jewish customs. As we talk, I turn my head toward the entrance of

the restaurant for a moment and notice a familiar-looking woman walk in. It takes me a minute, but then I place her.

"That's Naftali Fraenkel's mom!" I whisper to my friends. The mother of one of the boys who was kidnapped and murdered earlier that summer. She wears a colorful *tichel* around her head, which is wrapped like a turban. I recognize her from two videos. One where she petitioned the U.N. to help find the boys, before their bodies were discovered; and the other just recently, in which she addressed the Jewish world before Rosh Hashanah. With a smile on her face, she explained how her son's kidnapping and death brought the Jewish world together in an unbelievable way and how we must stay united as a people.

"I need to say something to her," I tell them. They look at me as if I'm crazy.

"What are you going to say?"

Before my nerves claim the better of me, I get up and approach her table.

"Excuse me, are you Naftali Fraenkel's mom?" I ask.

She nods her head. "*Ken.*" Yes.

"I'm so sorry for your loss… I just want to say that you are one of the strongest people I know. That you were able to inspire the Jewish world through your personal tragedy… I found it very inspiring. Thank you." She takes my hands in hers and tears well up for us both. Up close, I can see now how much pain resides behind her smile, the same warm smile I saw online.

"*Todah rabbah.*" Thank you, she whispers.

CHAPTER 38
Too Educated?

"TELL ME WHAT YOU ARE looking for," the matchmaker says, her notebook out with my name at the top of the page.

"I'm looking for someone who is serious about Torah learning and personal growth, but who will also have a profession and work full-time." She nods her head. Obviously, I say, *middos*, or good character traits, are a must. Ideally, he will also be musical and have a good sense of humor.

She sits in thought for a few moments. I'm anxious to hear if she has anyone in mind for me.

"Penn Law…" she says, smiling. Her pen taps on the notepad.

"Yes," I say, acknowledging the prestige of my degree.

"Most guys are not going to like this," she says. "They'll be intimidated by it. Especially guys who are serious about Torah. They want a woman who is going to prioritize the home."

"I definitely intend to do that," I assure her. I explain that I do not want to climb the corporate ladder, as Penn Law may suggest. I expect this to satisfy her, but it does not. She continues to harp on this stain on my dating resume, despite the fact that she knows guys who, like me, are American, educated, and have become religious. I sit there, deflated. For the rest of the meeting, I spend every last ounce of my energy trying to keep it together.

The moment I walk out of the meeting I burst into tears. I cry the whole ten-minute walk down to the bus stop.

I feel sorry for myself. This is surely the plight of a modern religious woman. If I were a man, Penn Law would be a gold star. But wait a minute. Where is my *emunah*? I know with all my heart that I was meant to go to Penn Law. I grew so much in my Yiddishkeit there. Would G-d lead me to Penn if it meant disqualification in the running for a good religious guy? I don't think so. I tell myself what I always have: that G-d made me, so surely there is a man out there who suits me. If a guy is intimidated by Penn Law, then clearly he is not the right one for me. I am disappointed in this matchmaker for inviting my old friends Fear and Doubt into the conversation when they had no place there. It's one thing to point out a potential issue, but to contrive that it's a deal breaker? I know then that my husband will have to come via a different messenger. But he seems farther away than ever now.

I walk out of my apartment in Nachlaot, music playing through my earbuds. I'm filled with a sense of purpose as I walk past the Machaneh Yehuda market and head toward the street-level light-rail train. I get off a quick two stops later at city hall. When I cross the street, my feet slide on the slippery Jerusalem stone that marks the outskirts of the Old City.

Walking alongside the ancient outer walls of the Old City toward Jaffa Gate, I feel the wind of the cool desert night against my face and readjust my headband over my ears to keep them covered. All types of people walk alongside me: tourists, Jews, Muslims. We are all brought here to Hashem's capital, as my mom half-jokingly refers to Jerusalem, for similar reasons. These reasons simultaneously unite us and separate us.

Passing through Jaffa Gate, I enter the Old City. The small courtyard is lined with tourist shops that sell religious souvenirs, colorful knitted bags, and scarves. Tourists study maps and figure out their next move. I slip past them and continue on my familiar route. Instead of going straight into the Muslim quarter of the Old City, which is the most direct route, I turn right and walk through the Jewish quarter. Palestinians have been committing more and more terrorist attacks against Jews in Jerusalem lately — I need to be careful. Yet the fear I know I should feel is tempered by a strong anticipation and the sense that I am somehow being protected.

I keep to the far left of the street to let cabs and cars pass by on the old narrow road that was never designed for modern traffic. I am relieved when I can veer left and head into a side alley, taking me officially into the Jewish quarter. A few Jews and tourists walk alongside me, in front of me, and behind me; we make up a stream flowing down the same current, through the winding alleyways that all lead down to the Kotel, the Western Wall.

As I weave my way through the narrow alleys in the quiet night, I marvel at the small, ancient stone buildings draped in vines and soft lights. I feel alone and yet also profoundly connected to my ancestors who walked this same path and my children and grand-children who will, G-d willing, walk it as well. I hear the whispers, the prayers, the laughs, and the cries of my people.

My excitement grows as I head down into Hurva Square, the larger courtyard at the heart of the Jewish quarter, which is sur-rounded by restaurants and shops. Religious children in uniforms play, while people sit and chat at an outdoor café. I pass the pizza store and Burgers Bar, the smell of fried goodness flowing through me for a few pleasant moments.

I quickly continue down the many stairs toward security. The stairs are lined with people asking for money. *Not again*, I think. I am slightly ashamed, but I always find this awkward. If I give to everyone each week, I'll be broke! Nonetheless, I always give a few shekels each visit to get in the habit of being a giver. The woman with the familiar weathered skin and a scarf on her head thanks me and gives me a blessing. But actually, I know she actually gave more to me than I gave to her, because she has just allowed me to perform the mitzvah of tzedakah, or charity. I know that mitzvot in this world cannot be measured by anything worldly, not all the money in the world. Surely a mitzvah is worth a few shekels! Plus, I try to give tzedakah before I pray, so that my prayers will be more readily answered. In the merit of opening my hand to others, I hope that Hashem will respond in kind and open His hand to me.

Between the two staircases there is a plateau, and I stop for a moment. There it is, in the distance: the Kotel. The Jerusalem-stone wall is covered in scattered vines and bushes that grow between the ancient bricks. Lit up by bright white nightlights, it stands there so humbly, yet with so much grandeur. This is my place. It's the first place I visit when I come to Israel and the last place I visit before I leave.

I continue down the rest of the stairs and pass through the turnstile into the security room, where I put my bag on a conveyor belt and walk through a metal detector. Before I know it, I am here. The large tiled plaza stretches before me.

It's not so crowded on this November night. To the right of the *mechitzah* divider, women bunch together close to the Kotel, with empty plastic chairs scattered behind them and their heads buried in their prayer books. Some of them sway, while others rock as they whisper their prayers. A few are crying. I try not to stare at their intimacy. There aren't many tourists stuffing notes into cracks in the walls. No, most of the women here tonight are regulars. Their relationship with G-d isn't an occasional "drop me a line" kind of thing; it's more a constant conversation, like you have with a beloved father or best friend.

I approach the wall slowly, out of respect. G-d's presence still rests in this place, though not in its former, revealed glory. I find a chair as close to the wall as I can get. I sit and take a few moments to prepare myself by saying a few psalms, poems King David composed to G-d. Then I rise and press my face and hands against the smooth, cool cracked stone. And I cry. This is the moment I've been waiting for, and I let it all go and sob for a while. When I am ready to speak, I cup my hands around my face, still pressed into the wall, and talk to G-d.

As is customary, I begin by blessing Him. "Bless You, Hashem, for watching over Israel, for watching over my family, for watching over me..."

Then I ask for help. "Hashem, help me. What is my life? Where do I go from here? Guide me, show me. Help me to have clarity, please. I'm scared. I'm scared I won't fulfill my purpose in this life. Please help me meet someone who really gets me, the right person to spend my life with. Please help me find him soon and smoothly." I pray for my friends, my family, the Jewish people, the world.

Last, I thank Him. "Thank You, Hashem, for keeping Israel safe, for watching over my family and me, for our health, for bringing me to Jerusalem..."

I know that to be a Jew in Jerusalem is a privilege. The Jews have been expelled from Jerusalem several times — by the Babylonians in the times of the First Temple, and then by the Romans during the period of the Second Temple, bringing us into our current two-thousand-year-old exile. Yet the Babylonians and the Romans did not act on their own; G-d used them as conduits to exile us, because for various reasons *we* were not fit as a nation to merit His presence in the Holy Temple in Jerusalem during those times. And we still are not, which is why we are reduced to praying at an outer wall of the Temple to beg for the inevitable redemption, when a Third Temple will be rebuilt.

After my prayers, as is the custom, I walk backward all the way out of the plaza, my eyes still on the wall so that I don't turn my back to G-d's presence.

On my walk home I feel lighter. I have a deep sense of peace that G-d has heard my prayers, and I have heard Him. *Everything will be okay.*

CHAPTER 39

Har Nof Attack

November 2014

ON THE MORNING OF MY twenty-fifth birthday, I sit up and recite *Modeh Ani. Thank You for restoring my soul within me. Thank You for another day of life.*

I eagerly check my messages. Instead of the birthday wishes I expected, my friend texts me: "There was a terror attack this morning at a shul in Har Nof. Five men were killed. One of the terrorists is still on the loose. Stay inside."

I stare at the message and try to absorb it. "One of the terrorists is still on the loose. Stay inside."

I can't believe what I am reading. Everyone I know has spoken of Har Nof as a safe haven in a turbulent country. No more, it seems. Our illusions are shattered. I sit there awhile, staring into space, paralyzed by the news.

Finally, I get up and mechanically go through the motions of my morning routine. As far as I know, I still have work.

I sit at our small wooden kitchen table and sip my breakfast shake, staring into space. Time seems to slow down. Only the horns of the cars and buses on the street below remind me that I need to keep moving. That's what people in Israel do, I guess. Yet reporting to work, business as usual, just doesn't seem right to me. It doesn't seem fair to them.

In the court, I sit at my desk and stare at my laptop. One by one my coworkers arrive. Michelle, who sits next to me, wishes me a happy birthday.

"Thanks," I answer, a bit embarrassed, "but I don't really feel like celebrating today."

"Why?" she asks.

I look at her. "Did you hear about the attack?"

"Yeah," she says. "Terrible."

After a moment of silence, she turns back to her laptop. *That's it?* I think. I struggle to maintain my composure. My coworkers chat and laugh as they type away on their keyboards. They discuss going to the movies and where to have lunch. I want to shout, "How dare you? How can you proceed as if everything's normal?" Yet I know that denial is easier — and perhaps even more productive — than facing the fear of yet another terror attack, of something so out of our control.

I leave my desk; I need some privacy. I lock myself in a bathroom stall, sit on the cold tile floor, scrunch my knees into my chest, bury my head, and sob.

After a while, I know I must return to my desk. I leave the bathroom and enter the sunlit halls lined with ancient Jerusalem stone. Court personnel walk past me quickly, absorbed in their daily responsibilities. They carry the weight of upholding democracy in Israel, and they must keep going. I want to tell them that it's not enough. That this conflict is as old as the stone on the walls, and it requires more of us. I return to my seat and pass the time until it is late enough to call America. On the roof of the courthouse, in a private corner, I sob to my parents like a baby.

I decide I need a break from the looming threat of a terror attack. When my clerkship at the court finishes, I return home for a break.

In New York, I spend Shabbos with the Moskowitzes. We have Friday night dinner at their neighbors the Bortzes, a beautiful, warm family that has also opened their home and heart to me over the years. Their Hungarian grandmother, Nanu, is a Holocaust survivor. After the seudah, Nanu asks me to come downstairs with her.

"This is *Perek Shirah*," she explains in her thick Hungarian accent, showing me a worn book with animals on the cover. The Song of Creation. "Say this each day for forty days," she instructs me, "to find a *shidduch*." I decide to take it on; I have nothing to lose.

The following week, I spend Shabbos in Philadelphia with the Lynns. When I go upstairs to my usual room and begin to unpack, I spot a small book sitting on the desk. I pick it up and can't believe my eyes — it's an English translation of *Perek Shirah*! Only once I see the book do I remember that I had forgotten to bring along my own copy. I have never noticed this book in their home until now.

Toward the end of Shabbos dinner, after the younger children drift off to play or sleep, I discuss my latest issues with Rabbi Lynn and Ruthi. Already I am thinking about next year. Where should I live when I move back from Israel? What type of job should I look for? What should I look for in a husband? Though Rabbi Lynn and Ruthi offer their usual sage advice, the future inevitably remains unclear.

After the meal, I sit on the couch to say *Perek Shirah* before I go to sleep. My eyes heavy, I mumble my way through it, page after page. When I finish, I realize that everyone has gone up to bed except Rabbi Lynn. "Good Shabbos," he says, as he starts up the stairs. Then he stops and turns toward me. "Did I tell you what my rabbi taught me about *Perek Shirah*?" he says. I shake my head no. "What's amazing about *Perek Shirah* is that each animal, each part of creation, has its own song. Its own song," he repeats, so that the words can sink in. "You have your own song, Jenna," he assures me. "Your own *tafkid*, purpose, in life. And you will find it, but it takes time. Ruthi and I are just figuring out our purpose now."

We both laugh. To think that I can figure things out so clearly at such a young age! Still, I can't help but try. As a planner, I want my path in life to be the most efficient. But Rabbi Lynn is telling me that life isn't like that. I need to live, to go on my journey step by step, and in doing this, my purpose will unfold naturally. Calm settles in me as I begin to accept the unknown, perhaps for the first time in my life. Upstairs, I lie on my bed in the dark, quiet room, tears of happiness streaming down my cheeks.

CHAPTER 40

The Last Flight Out

January 2015

BEFORE I AM MEANT TO fly back to Israel, I catch a bad case of the flu. I have no choice but to postpone my flight. My parents make a meager attempt to persuade me to stay and look for a job, but I refuse. The whole reason I wanted to go to Israel in the first place was to study in seminary, and I have yet to do that. When my mom sees how energized I am for the first time in days upon rebooking my flight, she doesn't have the heart to push the matter any further.

I spend the remaining two weeks in bed. One day, out of the blue, I receive an email from Rabbi Styne: "Shalom, Jenna. When are you coming back to Israel? I have a great *shidduch* idea I want to talk about with you when you get back." I answer him right away that I will be back soon and will be in touch then. I want to know more details about the guy, but I know I have to wait.

The day my flight is scheduled to leave for Israel, there's a bad snowstorm. Almost every flight leaving JFK Airport that day is cancelled — almost every flight except my own, that is, on good old El Al Airlines, which sticks to its schedule. There is some delay in the airport, and when we board the plane it is snowing hard. The windows are sprayed to prevent ice freeze. People in their seats wonder if we are actually going to take off in this weather. And then, to our amazement, our plane takes off in the midst of the snowstorm, the only one to fly out of JFK that night.

Back in Israel, in the *sherut* van to Jerusalem, I get an email from
Rabbi Styne: "Hi, Jenna, just checking in. Are you back in Israel
yet?" We schedule a time to speak later that night. Even though
I'm jet-lagged, I cannot wait to hear about the guy Rabbi Styne
has in mind for me.

"He's a spiritual lawyer, just like you," Rabbi Styne tells me that
night. Justin is from California and also came to study in Israel
after law school. "He is always positive. He plays guitar and does
yoga, yet he's also down-to-earth and responsible."

"That all sounds great," I say. "I'd love to meet him." Rabbi Styne
says he will send me Justin's dating resume when we hang up, so
I can learn more about him for myself. A few minutes later Rabbi
Styne does just that, signing off with a "Welcome home."

The top of Justin's resume has the usual: family background,
education, age, and so on. He's two and a half years older than me.
I like that he is a younger brother to an older sister; I am an older
sister to a younger brother. Then it gets more personal, as he describes himself and what he seeks in a spouse:

> *I am looking for someone warm and loving, with whom I can
> have a deep and intimate connection. There should always be
> a deep, unbreakable bond spiritually, emotionally, and physi-
> cally that transcends any circumstances. I envision us constant-
> ly giving to each other and constantly interested in knowing
> each other on a deeper level. Also, a commitment to personal
> growth is very important to me, striving to be better to each
> other, friends, family, and in our commitment to Hashem.*
>
> *I would like someone who will be a warm and caring moth-
> er, although with enough strength of character to keep an or-
> derly home, with discipline and respect. I would like to find
> someone who thinks deeply about life and Hashem, who has
> a rich inner world and a passion for learning and spirituality.*

Lastly, I would like to find someone who has a true simchat hachaim, an unwavering positivity and joy for life, a genuine happiness.

As I read Justin's vision for a marriage, I am immensely moved. Finally, someone who is not content with superficiality or even mediocrity, but strives to always go deeper. I want the same. Yet I know from experience that just because we seem to match on paper doesn't mean I should get too hyped up. Lower expectations are always better, I've learned. There is serious potential here, which is great, but I won't know any more until I meet him in person. Anyway, that's what I tell myself. More than once.

I email Rabbi Styne that I am eager to meet Justin. We set a date for the following Sunday night.

In the meantime, I get a call from Rabbi Miller,[*] from another yeshivah. When I had first moved to Israel, he said he had a guy in mind for me. We agreed that when the guy was ready to date, we would give it a try. Well, he says with excitement, the guy is ready to date and wants to meet me.

Uh-oh. I explain to Rabbi Miller the situation. But he does not want to take no for an answer. He tells me that this is the best guy in his yeshivah, and if I don't take the opportunity to meet him now it may not come around again. I tell him I will think about it and call him back.

I think the matter over and realize that Rabbi Miller never told me *why* this guy was specifically a good fit for me; he just said he's a great guy. There are a lot of great guys. Justin sounds perfect for me. In my heart, I know I need to meet him. If it doesn't work out with Justin and the other guy is no longer available, then clearly he is not meant for me.

---

[*] Name has been changed to protect privacy.

I tell Rabbi Miller that I am sorry, but I need to trust my gut on this one.

CHAPTER 41

The First Date

February 8, 2015

As I walk down the familiar path from the train station to Mamilla Mall, my heart has somehow gravitated to the pit of my stomach. It's a chilly February night, but my palms are sweaty in my jacket pockets. I adjust my knit headband over my blown-out hair. I feel pretty. I feel vulnerable. My boots click on the stones as I make my way. Suddenly I run into an acquaintance, a close friend of my roommate Shayna. Despite my attempts to keep my meeting with Justin private, I confess that I am going on a date.

"A first date?" she asks, grinning.

"Yes," I say, with a slight smile.

"You look beautiful." We hug and part ways. As I walk, I play some upbeat music and try to talk myself down. I remember something I had learned recently: You can achieve more by trying less. I don't need to win Justin. I need to be myself. If he doesn't like me, then he is not the right one for me. *That's it.* Oh, how I wish the heart spoke logic! Though if it did, it might be a colder, duller world.

As I enter Mamilla Mall, my heart thumps more loudly. It's two minutes past eight. Is he already there?

I approach Café Café. I see a guy wearing a suit and black *kippah*, facing the opposite store, which happens to be called Ahava, or Love. Although I've only seen a picture of his face, I know it's Justin. I give myself a moment before I walk over. Standing there,

I think, *My life might never be the same again.*

He turns around and our eyes meet. I walk toward him. "Justin?"

"Hi." He smiles. He is cute.

"Is it okay that we're meeting here? I know I suggested this place, but we can go somewhere else if you prefer," I say, rattling on a mile a minute. He laughs.

"This is great," he assures me. We walk into the warmly lit outdoor tent, set up for winter, and take a table in the corner. There are only a few other people here tonight. We order two hot drinks, herbal tea for me and a sweet vanilla coffee drink for him.

I tell him about my recent trip back to America and how I got the flu. "I bless you that you should never get the flu," I say, half-joking.

"A blessing from a *tzedekes*," he says. I laugh at his referring to me as a righteous woman. The compliment feels good.

"So you're a lawyer too," Justin begins, smiling. He has beautiful, straight white teeth.

"A lawyer by training, but I'm really a writer at heart," I answer, surprised by my newfound confidence. I had never really called myself a writer before.

"Really? That's so cool. What type of stuff do you like to write?"

Nonfiction, I tell him, though I explain how I am discovering my writer's voice for the first time. He asks me why I went to law school. I tell him about my passion for climate change.

"But ultimately, my family pressured me to go," I tell him.

"Me too," he says. "That's the path, right? Go to college and then become a doctor or lawyer… I'm actually also an artist at heart. A musician."

"Right! Rabbi Styne mentioned that you play the guitar?"

"Yes."

"That's awesome," I say. We discuss our favorite artists for a while. It turns out that we like a lot of the same music. The waiter brings our hot drinks in large white mugs. Justin says a blessing with concentration and then takes a small sip from his steaming drink.

"So," he says, leaning forward, "tell me about your spiritual journey. Did it start at Emory?" I begin to tell him how I began by looking into Buddhism and Transcendental Meditation. "No way! Me too!" he says. "The first Jewish book I read was *Letters to a Buddhist Jew*."

"Me too!" I say. We talk about the appealing aspects of Buddhism, and how we found them in Judaism. How hard it was for us at first to identify as a Jew coming from a universal perspective. I go on to describe my serendipitous Israel trip and my determination to continue learning when I got back to America. As I talk, he listens intently with a big smile. It's sweet.

I continue my story, briefly, though with enough detail for him to appreciate the nuances. Along the way, Justin shares his story. He began searching spiritually in law school. He practiced meditation and yoga regularly. Then a Persian Jewish friend from law school, Joe, encouraged him to do a ten-week program with a rabbi in Los Angeles, which culminated in a free trip to Israel over their December break. Like me, Justin was blown away by the depth and relevance of Jewish wisdom. He continued to learn on his own when he returned to Los Angeles.

"I decided to come back to Israel to study in yeshivah for three months while I waited for my bar results," he tells me. "But once I got here, I was hooked and knew I had to stay. Three months turned into one year, and one year turned into two."

"Wow. That's amazing." I tell him how I wanted to study at Neve for the year after college, but my family insisted that I come back and start law school. I'm worried he will judge me for this, but he totally understands.

"My family wasn't happy that I decided to stay in yeshivah," he admits. We talk about our families, how they are supportive but don't really understand what we're doing here. How can they?

As we talk, the staff begins to stack chairs on the tables. Finally, a waiter places a bill between us.

"It looks like they're closing up," I say.

"What time is it?" Justin asks. We realize we have been talking for well over three hours. I wish the restaurant wasn't closing.

We walk out of Mamilla Mall and share a cab. When the driver stops to drop me off, Justin steps outside as well. We smile at each other and say good night. There are no promises of a second date. Rabbi Styne will let me know if Justin wants to go out again. But I think we both know that we will meet again.

Right when I get home, I email Rabbi Styne. "I think Justin is awesome. I would like to see him again, and hopefully he does too." That night I have trouble falling asleep, I am so excited.

The next morning, during a break between classes, I check my email. Rabbi Styne writes back, "Justin thinks *you* are awesome." From the moment I see those words, I am on cloud nine. We are going to meet that Wednesday night for another date.

CHAPTER 42

The Same Neshamah

ON OUR SECOND DATE, JUSTIN and I meet at Fresh Kitchen, a restaurant in the old train station. The last time I had been there was the previous fall, when I met Cynthia for dinner. During our meal, two young Arab boys threw a hand grenade into the courtyard outside the restaurant just a few feet away, and it sounded like a bomb. The restaurant went quiet; everyone was stunned for a moment. When an older Israeli woman started to cry, I began to panic. I became dizzy and disoriented. Cynthia assured me that it wasn't an actual bomb. Still, it was enough to have kept me away from the old train station ever since.

When Rabbi Styne tells me Justin wants to meet at that same restaurant, I hesitate, but in the end I agree. I know it's good for me to return to the same spot and have what I hope will be a positive experience.

After we order hot drinks and a piece of chocolate lava cake, I tell Justin what happened to me here. He asks if I want to go somewhere else, but I tell him that I'm okay.

"Tell me about your parents," he begins. "What are they like? What about them do you want to emulate?" I like that he has questions prepared.

As I begin to answer, the cake comes. "If I get chocolate on my teeth, you have to tell me," I say with a smile. He agrees.

We talk about our families, whom we are both close with. Justin's parents are American, like mine. He tells me more about his mother's Ashkenazi Hungarian background and his father's Sephardic Middle Eastern background, which explains his olive-toned skin and nearly black hair. As I begin to talk about my great-grandparents and where they came from, I'm afraid to bore him with the details. But Justin's eyes are alight, as usual, and he asks me question after question. It turns out we both have a strong interest in family ancestry, in reconnecting to our lineage.

The second date goes as smoothly as the first. We meet the following Sunday for a third date, this time at the Israel Museum. Before each date I battle with my nerves, but once Justin and I are together, we invariably assume a natural flow. We open up more about our childhoods, our interests, our goals and dreams. We share funny stories and make jokes.

"How is the *shidduch* going?" Ruthi asks me on the phone.

"Ruthi!" I say. "It's crazy! We are the same *neshamah*, the same soul."

"Jenna. You are not the same *neshamah*," she says, laughing.

"Ruthi! We are!"

"Don't start imagining the wedding chuppah just yet. Take your time, see where things go."

I know Ruthi is right. I need to stay grounded. But I feel in my heart that this could be it.

As I realize that I have never met a guy with whom I have connected as deeply as Justin — and after only a few dates, no less — I become frightened. What if he decides he doesn't want to continue and it ends just like that, with a call from Rabbi Styne? The thought itself is enough to make me sick. I feel myself shutting down. I don't want to open up anymore. But I know that I have to. It's the only way we can know if we are right for each other. I need to let him see me.

Before our fourth date, I pray and say psalms in the cab, asking

G-d that we both continue to be our genuine selves. That we have clarity about each other and that it works out if it is the right thing.

We meet at an upscale Italian restaurant. It's our first dinner date. Justin asks me about my vision for the home, for raising children. I am relieved that he also wants his children to get a secular education, to have the option of a profession if they choose to pursue one. But we agree that Torah needs to be the center of the home. In the spaces between our conversations, we look at each other and smile.

On the walk home, in a brave moment, I confess to Justin that it's hard for me to open up when I know that Rabbi Styne could just tell me no and I would never see him again. I ask him if at this point, he could speak to me directly if he has any concerns or if he doesn't want to go out again, and not rely on the *shadchan*, or matchmaker, to relay that message. He agrees.

I am relieved when after the fifth date Rabbi Styne gives Justin my number. We still consult with him in between dates, but Justin calls me to arrange our dates now. He picks me up at the corner of my alleyway. As I walk up the narrow road to meet him, he stands there, smiling.

Soon we exchange emails and begin to share things. He sends me a picture of his family. I figure this is a good sign, and I tell my parents and my grandpa that I am seeing someone. The religious dating process moves so quickly, I need to give them enough time to digest this information in case it does turn into something more serious. I give minimal information, though. I simply say that I'm dating someone, an American lawyer. Despite my mom's probing questions, I tell her it's not worth discussing further at this point.

I remember the words of Rabbi Shlomo Carlebach, who said that when two people are right for each other, what is special about each of them is the same; they share the same specialness. The more Justin and I share, the more it becomes clear that we are not getting to know each other for the first time, but that we are revealing two parts of the same soul. A soul that has been split, living parallel lives on opposite coasts of the U.S. We have the same fears and the same yearnings. We both want the most out of life. We both want to live with authenticity, integrity, and intention and do not want to settle for anything less. We love art and spiritual growth, yet are practical and responsible.

Each morning as I walk from the train station to seminary and replay parts of our dates in my mind, I melt. I attempt to put myself back together again for classes, where as far as most of my friends are concerned, I have not met the man I think is my soul mate. There is a Jewish idea that blessing comes in secret, and I take this seriously. Until there is an engagement, there is nothing to talk about in public. Yet I can't help but break down and share my sweet secret with two of my closest friends in seminary, and of course my roommate Shayna. Throughout the day, despite how engaging my classes are, my thoughts always come back to Justin.

CHAPTER 43

Behind the Mask

AFTER I HAVE BEEN DATING Justin for a few weeks, Illana visits Israel on a *chizuk* mission, an inspirational trip for women. She invites me to spend Shabbos with her at their hotel in Jerusalem. Shira Smiles, an American Torah teacher living in Israel, will be the honored guest. I jump at the chance to spend Shabbos with Illana and hear one of my favorite teachers speak.

After Shabbos dinner, the women make their way downstairs to a small conference room, where Rebbetzin Smiles speaks about the upcoming holiday of Purim, and specifically about Hashem's involvement in our lives.

"In the Purim story," she explains, "the Jews had distanced themselves from G-d, so He responded in turn. G-d relates to us how we relate to Him. If man wishes to distance himself from G-d and feels that he is independent, then G-d will allow him to perceive — however falsely — that he is alone…

"The illusion of G-d's hiddenness in the Purim story is what makes it so powerful. Even when events seem like natural coincidences, in reality G-d is orchestrating every detail of our national and personal lives beyond our wildest imaginations…"

Her words hit me like a lightning bolt. Sometimes we have heard an idea before, but because we have changed, the way we process the same idea is radically different. I have learned about Divine Providence, but tonight, Shira Smiles's words speak to my heart in the most intimate way. I feel as if she is speaking directly to me; that I was meant to hear these words.

I sit in my chair, tears streaming down my cheeks. "Are you okay?" Illana whispers. I assure her that I am, but I'm so overwhelmed with emotion that I need to leave. I get up and find the nearest bathroom, which thankfully is empty. I grab a bunch of tissues and sink onto the tiled floor. I realize this isn't my first time sitting on the floor of a bathroom in Israel crying. But this time, my mascara-stained tears are not ones of sadness and confusion but of joy and clarity.

I finally understand. Why I got rejected from my Birthright trip, why I had to struggle with my parents and my grandpa, why I needed to start law school when I did, why I was rejected by Ben, why I didn't get any of the jobs I applied to after graduation. The suffering that I endured was painful, but I realize now, for the first time, in my heart, that it was necessary and for my greatest good.

I see now that at times when G-d felt distant, like when I was in the Bahamas or when I dated Adam, it was because I had pulled away from Him. Other times I sought connection with G-d but still felt in the dark. I remember arguing with my parents at the Bob Dylan concert. Praying to G-d in my law school apartment for direction. I see behind the mask now; G-d was with me the entire time.

I feel as if I am standing on the peak of a mountain, overlooking the timeline of my life and seeing all of the dots connect in the most seamless and intricate manner, building up to this moment. Everything that I went through needed to happen for me to be here, right now, on the bathroom floor in Jerusalem, with the clarity that I have found my soul mate.

PART III

TRANSCENDENCE

CHAPTER 44

A Real Jewish Princess

WHEN I FIRST MEET RABBI Yitzchak Joshua, one of Justin's rabbis from yeshivah, he looks into my eyes for a while. One might find him intimidating at first, a Sephardic Englishman with a long beard dressed in a black suit and black hat. But his warm smile and sparkling eyes put me at ease immediately.

Apparently, Rabbi Joshua can discern information about a person simply by looking at his face. A few weeks ago, Justin showed him a picture of my family and me, and everything he said about us was on point. Tonight, outside the ice cream shop, as Rabbi Joshua looks into my eyes for those few long moments, I know that he can see through me and into the depths of my soul. I let him in. I know I'm not perfect, I tell myself, but my essence is good. I have nothing to hide. When he diverts his eyes, I know the meeting is essentially over and the rest mere formalities.

As we sit around a table outside and eat our ice cream, Rabbi Joshua talks about marriage. "A soul mate is not just someone to spend this life with; your souls are bound in the afterlife." Justin and I glance at each other and smile.

"Don't scare him, Rabbi!" I joke. We all laugh.

The next night, Justin and I meet outside the home of his *rosh yeshivah* for another meeting.

"I spoke to Rabbi Joshua today," Justin tells me.

"Oh yeah?" I ask. "What did he say?"

"He really liked meeting you. I want to tell you all about it, but I know we have to go in now. I just want to tell you one thing he said first."

"What?" I ask, smiling.

"He said I have a real Jewish princess."

"What did he say?" I ask again. I need to make sure I am not imagining this.

"He said I have a real Jewish princess."

CHAPTER 45

We Are "Us" Now

ONE *MOTZA'EI SHABBOS,* JUSTIN AND I sit at Café Rimon in Mamilla Mall. "Would you move to LA?" he asks me.

Before Justin and I met, I had asked Rabbi Styne where Justin wanted to live. He told me that he planned to move back to LA, where he had gone to law school, but that he was open. At the end of my year in Israel, I had planned to move back to New York. But that was before I met Justin…

Los Angeles. I had been to California only once before on a summer trip when I was in high school. I loved it. My friends and I dreamed of settling in California one day.

"Yes," I tell Justin, "I would." In my mind, this answer means: *I would theoretically move to LA.* In his mind, this answer means: *We will live in LA.* But in the moment, we are completely unaware of this miscommunication and are lost in each other's eyes, giddy at the prospect of an "us." A future together.

"I think he is the one," I tell my parents on the phone. It's been at least six weeks since I told them about Justin initially. I expect them to freak out, but they seem happy, even supportive. After all, he seems to fit the bill. He's American, he's a lawyer, he plans to move back to America and work. For these reasons, my grandpa also approves. Of course, I don't mention to him that Justin is religious. Nor do I mention anything about us potentially moving to LA. It doesn't seem so relevant anyway, as we plan to spend at least the first year of marriage in Israel so we can continue our learning. I don't mention that to anyone, either. Not yet.

Things move quickly. Before I know it, we are Skyping with each other's parents and siblings.

"I can't believe I'm my meeting my future son-in-law for the first time on Skype," is all my mom can say. What can we do? We have a trip to America planned during Pesach to meet our families, but that's still a few weeks away.

During Chol HaMoed Pesach, we fly to San Diego to meet Justin's family. We plan to spend a week in San Diego, followed by a week in New York at my parents' house. I know that Justin plans to propose on the trip, but I'm not sure when. During one of our recent dates, he told me that he called my parents to ask their permission to propose.

After a long day of traveling, I wake up in Justin's home in San Diego, jet-lagged but high on adrenaline. I'm impressed that his mom has turned over her house for Pesach, enough so that we could eat there. We are having brunch with his family when Justin asks if he could take me sailing. *Sailing?* I think. *Today?* I'm exhausted. "Sure," I say, not wanting to disappoint him.

When we get to the dock, he leads me to a sailboat covered in rose petals, chocolate-covered strawberries, and champagne. As I step onto the boat, I am shaking.

He takes me out into Mission Bay. It is a clear, sunny California spring day. After a while, he stops rowing. As the boat gently rocks, he takes out portable speakers from his backpack and begins to play soft music. He opens a jewelry box to reveal a diamond heart-shaped necklace.

"Jenna, I want to spend the rest of my life with you. Will you marry me?"

"Yes!" I tell him. I take out the necklace and put it on carefully. This is all so different from the way I thought I would get engaged.

But in this moment, it is perfect.

After the moment has passed, we stay put for a while, letting the waves sway us back and forth. We look at each other, filled with emotion and wearing big smiles, savoring the moment and everything that is to come.

We return to Justin's house to celebrate with his extended family. I FaceTime my parents to tell them the news. Amidst hugs and loud chatter, I show them my necklace. My mom seems upset. I go upstairs to the room where I am staying and close the door.

"No ring?" my mom says. "I don't understand." I explain to my mom that in Jewish tradition, it is customary for men to propose with another piece of jewelry. She is not satisfied. In her world, the only way to propose is with a ring and anything less is unacceptable.

"If he doesn't get you a ring, we are not making a wedding."

"Don't worry, Mom, he is going to get me a ring," I reassure her. Truthfully, Justin and I hadn't discussed it. I had expected a ring, but I later learn that one of Justin's rabbis advised him to get me another piece of jewelry instead. I was a bit disappointed, but I wasn't going to dwell on it. I had found my *bashert* — the person destined for me! That was the biggest blessing of all. Couldn't my mom see that?

A week later, Justin, my mom, and I ride the train into Manhattan. Our destination: the diamond district. Thankfully, Justin understood that my assimilated parents need to see a ring on my finger before they move forward. Within a few short hours, we are back on the train to Long Island, mission accomplished. Don't get me wrong, I love the ring. But I didn't have the luxury of time and so I picked one of the first few we saw.

That night, we have a *vort*, an engagement party, at my parents' home. When the Lynns arrive at the door, Ruthi and I burst into tears of joy. Rabbi Lynn speaks to a crowd of mostly secular Jews. "This is actually not normal," he says. "That people like Jenna and Justin, who are so, well, normal, can make such brave and courageous decisions and find each other so quickly and so beautifully and connect on such a deep level. I'm telling you; I do this for a living. This is unique and this is special." Justin and I look at each other, starry-eyed.

And so, I enter "Kallah Land" a place where you feel the highest highs and, due to the stress of making a wedding, can feel the lowest lows.

We want to get married before the Three Weeks, the period of mourning commemorating the destruction of the first and second Temples. *Baruch Hashem*, a nearby hotel has a cancellation for June 28, the last Sunday before the Three Weeks. That gives us a little over two months to make the wedding. However, I'm planning on going back to Israel with Justin for the majority of the engagement.

During the week we are in New York, I ask a religious mentor where to buy a sheitel. I should ask her to come with me, but I'm in such a rush to get as much done as possible that I don't want to accommodate her schedule. So off I go to the *sheitel macher*, wig stylist, with my mom, who never wore a wig in her life. Both of us are clueless. I naively think that I have to get the most expensive type of sheitel. The *sheitel macher* puts a beautiful European wig on my head and pulls out some of my hair in the front. As weird as it feels to be wearing a wig, the hair looks very natural, almost like my own. I immediately give her a down payment.

A few days later, I return with my mom so the *sheitel macher* can cut it. While she snips away at the sheitel, she chats with another customer who just came in. My mom and I look at each other in disbelief. How can this woman not pay 100 percent attention when she is cutting such an such an expensive wig?!

When I return home, I anxiously try on the wig, this time without pulling my own hair in the front. It looks nothing like it did in the store. I feel ridiculous, like I'm entering the next beauty pageant. I stare at myself, almost unable to recognize my own reflection. Tears well up in my eyes.

My mom begs me to stay in New York until the wedding, but I won't hear of it. For one, Justin and I feel like we need more time together as a couple before we get married. I also want to continue whatever I can of my Torah learning.

However, in hindsight, I wish I had spent more time at home before the wedding. Although in the religious world, making a wedding in two months is par for the course, in my parents' world, it was a major rush. After all, secular engagements last for at least a year. My parents had never even been to a religious wedding! And now they were making one for their only daughter, while she was halfway around the world.

I helped from Israel as much as I could. I left seminary early each day so that I could begin making phone calls first thing in the morning New York time. My parents, true music lovers, wanted to book a secular band with a female singer. I had to explain to them why this wouldn't work. Thankfully, we found a *frum* band that played both Jewish and secular music. My parents were as supportive as possible. They planned a totally kosher wedding, *mechitzah* and all. My mom would wear a modest gown. I really couldn't have asked for anything more.

But as supportive as they were, they continued to question everything. Was Justin really the right guy for me? Was this really the life I wanted to lead? Although they liked Justin, they didn't really know him yet. They were uncomfortable at the idea of making a wedding when they hardly knew him or his family. I couldn't blame them. Nevertheless, I continued to reassure them, and we went ahead.

My mom had waited her whole life to plan my wedding with me. In returning to Israel, I had robbed her of the experience she longed for: Slowly putting together the registry. Shopping around for a dress. Taste-testing until we found the perfect caterer. Instead, everything was rushed, and I made every decision as quickly as possible. It wasn't what I had expected my engagement to look like, but truthfully, I wasn't one of those girls who dreamed about my wedding. Before I became *frum*, my dream was to change the world through a career. Marriage wasn't really on my radar. I thought maybe I would get married when I was thirty. And yet here I was, twenty-five years old, planning my wedding, grateful that G-d had intervened in my life so clearly and directed me to my *bashert*. The flowers, the cake, it's all just *gashmiyus*, physicality, I told myself. What really matters is getting married, not planning the wedding. But what I didn't understand was that to my mom it *did* matter. And so, it should have mattered more to me.

CHAPTER 46

Rain in Its Proper Time

"How everything comes together is what I want to talk about," Rabbi Styne begins, addressing the group at our *vort* in Israel. "How everything comes together between a bride and a groom. How everything comes together in this week's Torah portion, and how everything comes together on the perfect time and day.

"In this week's Torah portion, *Beha'alotecha* (Hebrew for 'When you step up'), G-d tells the Jewish people, 'If you walk in My ways then you will get rain in its time.' The Hebrew word for rain, *geshem*, also means *shefa*, a flow of blessing from above.

"The Sfas Emes explains that there are three expressions through which G-d sends his blessings in this world: time, place, and man. Everyone has the flow that he or she needs. There's an appropriate time for that flow and an appropriate location for that flow. The Sfas Emes says that if one walks the way of Torah, then he can merit to raise the three expressions of blessing to the point of unity and receive blessing at exactly the right time, in exactly the right place, with exactly the right person. In this way, he merits to see G-d, the Unified Source, behind the blessing.

"I have a lot of proofs that Justin and Jenna have been walking in the Torah's ways for quite a long time, and especially in these last couple of years," Rabbi Styne continues. "It's a good thing that I don't delete any of my emails." The crowd begins to laugh as Rabbi Styne takes papers out of his jacket pocket.

"It wasn't long ago that a young lady named Jenna sat with me in the hotel lobby of the Novotel. Jenna and I discussed the inspiration that she was feeling from the Israel trip, and how, exactly, was she going to explain that to her Long Island parents? Jenna came off that trip, and for most students the inspiration is gone almost immediately. But not for her.

"June 11, 2009. Jenna writes: 'Shalom, Rabbi Styne, I miss Israel *so* much!'" Everyone laughs, including me. My face is hot, and I rub my sweaty palms on my dress. "'I definitely still have some of the energy from the trip with me, but it's hard going from Israel to Long Island, as you know...' She describes how she got Shabbos candles, a mezuzah scroll, and some books to stay inspired. She writes, 'As of now, I know G-d is here...'

"Year after year I visited Jenna on campus and we sat in different student lounges, and I watched a young lady walking, and walking, and walking in the ways of Torah." I look down, fighting tears.

Thankfully, Rabbi Styne takes the spotlight off of me.

"It took him a while, but there was a young man named Justin who came to the yeshivah on his first Israel trip a few years ago. I followed up with an email when he returned to Los Angeles, and the next day he emailed me back: 'Yes, I am interested in studying at the yeshivah!' When he submitted his application, he explained that there was a 90 percent chance that he could only stay three months... Yes, there was actually a percentage." Everybody laughs. "Even though we are usually strict about attending the whole nine-month program the first year, I knew deep in my *kishkes,* my gut, that Justin was going to stay for more than three months.

"A few months ago, Justin walked into my office and said, 'I'm ready to date.' Jenna had come to my house three months earlier and told me she was ready to date. 'Jenna,' I told her, 'I don't have anyone for you yet.' 'Justin,' I said, 'two people already contacted me about you, and they each have an idea for you. I also have an idea for you.'"

Then, turning to the crowd, Rabbi Styne says, "But free will has to be preserved. I can't say, 'Justin, I have the girl for you,' because there's two other people who also think they have the girl for him, and he has to make the choice. So I send him three resumes, without any indication of who the three candidates came from. Justin calls me that night, out of breath, and says, 'I know which one is yours, and I think she is the one who is for me, and that's where I want to start.'

"Out of respect for their privacy, I am not going to read the emails that Justin and Jenna sent me between their dates, but their responses were almost identical each time; they are like two peas in a pod."

Justin and I make eye contact. My face hurts from smiling.

Rabbi Styne continues. "Justin gave me permission to recount the main ideas of what he was looking for in a spouse: a positive person, someone with whom he could build an intimate bond and trust, someone with a deep inner world, someone who is thoughtful, has a relationship with Hashem, is warm and motherly but has the strength to run a home, someone who is empathetic, compassionate, and sensitive. So many characteristics that are so big, so deep, so opposite from each other," he says, turning to Justin, "and she's sitting right across from you.

"Jenna's resume. She writes, 'I am looking for someone who is passionate about Judaism, growth oriented, and spiritual, but also grounded.' She wanted someone who was optimistic, compassionate, and musical, but also intellectual and driven. Again, the statistics of finding someone with all of these qualities, some of them in direct opposition to each other, is so rare. It doesn't happen." Rabbi Styne turns to me and says, "You are looking at him.

"If you walk in the ways of Torah…" Rabbi Styne continues. "I've watched these people, year after year, walking, and walking, and walking."

I remember that morning in the Bahamas. *Walking.* Getting on my first Israel trip. *Walking.* Fighting to go back to Neve. *Walking.* Struggling to make observance my own at Penn. *Walking.* Striving to get back to Israel after law school. *Walking.* Justin telling his family, who was eager for him to begin work, that he was going to yeshivah. *Walking.* That he was staying for the year. *Walking.* That he was going back for another year! *Walking.*

"We see here the flow of blessing came together at exactly the right time, in exactly the right place, between exactly the right people. At the end of their time here in Israel, they are going home to get married. Jenna and Justin, you two should merit to build the home that you dream of. If there is a match that I feel so good about from the bottom of my heart, it is this one. You should continue to bring us *nachas*, and we should continue to share in many simchahs, happy occasions, together."

"Amen!" everyone answers. I get up and hug my friends and teachers, still holding a bunch of raggedy wet tissues in one hand.

CHAPTER 47

Tov L'Hodos La'Hashem

WHEN I WAS SINGLE, I often dreamed about my *badeken* (veiling ceremony). Although I didn't know my *chassan* (groom) yet, just imagining the intensity of the moment brought me to tears.

And now here I am. My mom and grandma to my left. Justin's mom, grandma, and sister to my right. Ruthi Lynn, Illana Moskowitz, and other close mentors and friends behind me. As the men sing "*Od Yishama*" and escort Justin to the *badeken*, the energy gets higher and higher. The room is packed, filled with Jews of every walk of life. High school friends, college friends, and family members who have never witnessed such a scene in their lives. Justin's Sephardic side of the family, who can't imagine a wedding any other way. Our yeshivah and seminary friends, mentors, and rabbis, most of whom had a similar journey to Justin and me. But in this moment, none of these differences matter. We are all united in this awesome simchah.

At the urge of Rabbi Lynn, my dad steps forward. Unsure of himself, he takes a piece of paper out of his jacket pocket and reads the blessing. Tears come to my eyes. My sweet dad. He doesn't understand it, he doesn't relate to it. And yet he blesses me anyway from the bottom of his heart.

After Justin's father and grandfather come up to give their blessings, Justin steps up onto the platform with a big smile and everybody cheers. He carefully pulls the veil over my head. And just like that, it's over. The men whisk Justin off to the chuppah.

In my dressing room, Ruthi repeated how important it is that I daven with *kavanah* (concentration) under the chuppah. I had been davening all day for everything under the sun. Still, I know I need to focus now, regardless of how the spotlight makes me uncomfortable.

I walk to the chuppah to "*Tov L'Hodos*." The words from *Tehillim* (Psalms) that speak to me so deeply: "It is good to give thanks to Hashem, and to sing praises to Your Name. To tell of Your kindness in the morning, and of Your faithfulness in the nights." Ultimately, when I thought about the sentiment I wanted to express during this holy time, I wanted to thank Hashem and to publicly praise Him for all that He has done for me. Both in the "morning," when everything was clear and in the "nights," when I didn't have clarity, but Hashem was guiding me every step of the way.

I begin to circle around Justin. As we begin the process of two lives coming together, which is never easy, I know Justin and I will have challenges. Right now, our relationship is a gift. We did nothing to earn it. We will have to work on it. Only then can we achieve real love. It is the same pattern that my Jewish journey took; it is the same pattern as building anything: Experiencing the initial light or inspiration, struggling in the dark to live that inspiration, and finally making it your own — transcendence, as Rabbi Tatz calls it.

I know the work that lies ahead. But at this moment, as I stand beside Justin under the chuppah, I allow myself to feel the *nachas* of my own personal transcendence. I feel as if G-d is peeking out from behind His mask and winking at me, reassuring me that He has been walking with me the whole time, and will continue to walk with me, with us, in our lives together. That is enough.

My Breslov rebbetzin from Israel told me not to stop dancing at the wedding: Just dance! And dance we do. My secular friends, who were so careful to dress modestly for the occasion, join hand in hand with my seminary friends, circling around me to Jewish music they have never heard before. Together, they do shtick — performing entertaining routines on the dance floor to bring me joy — and elevate the simchah. My mom and I hold hands as we dance in the middle of the circle. Although she still questions everything, in this moment, she seems happy.

The day after the wedding, I receive an email from Randi, my college roommate. When I became religious, it was hard for her. This made her email all the more amazing: "You guys managed to create an atmosphere that seamlessly brought people together, regardless of their faith or familiarity with certain customs. I was so pleasantly surprised by how fun the whole night was, and how beautiful some of the traditions are…"

Upon reading the email, tears well up in my eyes (unsurprising, I know). I am so grateful that Justin and I were able to make a *kiddush Hashem*, a sanctification of G-d's Name, at the wedding.

CHAPTER 48

Shanah Rishonah

AFTER SHEVA BERACHOS, THE WEEK of festive meals following the wedding, Justin and I sit at the kitchen table with my parents. We can't put it off any longer; we need to tell them our plan to delay our move to Los Angeles and spend *shanah rishonah* in Israel. For most religious families, the first year of marriage in Israel is an encouraged rite of passage, viewed as a blessing. For my parents, it could not have been worse news. It's like telling them: We are going to postpone working, live in a war zone, and become even greater religious fanatics.

As we expected, they are shocked, hurt, and angry. "If we had known you were planning this, we would not have made you the wedding we did," they tell us. Their words sting. We try to explain ourselves, but we realize we made a grave error. While we thought we were saving everyone from unneeded stress during the engagement period, my parents felt like we were lying the entire time.

A few weeks later, we go to Lower Merion to celebrate the wedding of our close friends from seminary and yeshivah. Rabbi Styne is there as well. After the seudah, we take a long walk with him. As we walk through the dark, winding roads, we discuss the various factors at play: The benefit of a year of learning in Israel. The risk of pushing off another year of working. My grandpa. There is no way he will approve of this, and we fear our actions could have serious repercussions, not only for us but for my parents. In the end, Rabbi Styne feels that it would be best to move to LA and begin our lives there, as we told our families we would, and revisit spending time in Israel down the road.

We are disappointed, but we trust his *daas Torah*.

We find a backhouse to rent in La Brea, the community that Justin is most familiar with. I don't know anything from anything, having been to California only twice before the move. I have one friend from seminary who lives "on the other side of town," in Pico, but that's literally it. As we drive through the city, I keep thinking, *Why am I here?* I feel so…displaced. So alone. I left my entire life behind and have to start over. I try to occupy myself with cooking and learning and finding a job, but I can't stop crying. "What did I do? Why did I agree to this?"

"I have always felt like Hashem was with me, but since we came here, I can't see any *hashgachah*." My voice cracks as I speak to Rabbi Baruch Yehuda Gradon, who sits across from me in his sukkah. "It just seems so random. Like, why am I here? Is this where I'm really supposed to be?" It is ironic that in the sukkah, the very place that represents closeness to Hashem, that I realize I have never felt so alone.

A few days earlier, I was on the phone with Ruthi and Rabbi Lynn, describing how sad and disoriented I felt living in Los Angeles. Although I spent my post-high school years in different cities, it felt temporary, because I always planned to move back to New York. Now, I realized, I was never going home again. Our new life in LA felt so permanent and overwhelming.

"Jenna. You need to meet with Rabbi Gradon," they told me.

The Lynns are close to Rabbi Gradon, as Rabbi Lynn became religious in LA. I had heard about Rabbi Gradon at the Lynns'

Shabbos table many times. He is a *rosh kollel* (head of a yeshivah for advanced adult students) and one of the biggest rabbis in the city. I was intimidated to reach out, but I was desperate for some guidance.

Rabbi Gradon looks at me with his piercing blue eyes. "Hashem is always with you," he assures me. "And Justin is a genuine, good guy who just wants to do the right thing. I meet a lot of people. Believe me when I tell you that today, a guy like Justin is hard to find. He is a gem; he really is. And more than that, he suits you. Many men would be intimated by your intelligence and accomplishments, but Justin is proud of you. It is obvious... And based on what you told me about Justin's job prospects, it makes perfect sense why you are in Los Angeles."

For a moment, his words of clarity illuminate the dark path I have been walking. I realize how important it is to speak with an experienced, objective mentor, especially in times like these.

"As for where to live," Rabbi Gradon continues, "there is no question that you two need to move to Pico. There are a lot of young people there, especially *baalei teshuvah*. You will be able to make more of an impact." He takes out his phone and immediately sets us up in Pico that Shabbos.

CHAPTER 49

Planting Seeds (Again)

Fall 2015

A FEW MONTHS AFTER WE move to Pico, my grandpa passes away at the age of ninety-nine. He had been too frail to come to the wedding. It may have been a blessing; I don't think he really knew how religious our simchah was going to be. After the wedding, Justin and I traveled to Florida to visit him. He enjoyed meeting Justin. Perhaps now that Grandpa is in the next world, he understands the life we are living and appreciates the mitzvot we do for the aliyah of his *neshamah*, the elevation of his soul.

A month after Grandpa's passing, Justin finds a job in a firm in LA that focuses on intellectual property, his area of interest. The firm is high level, usually recruiting their new attorneys from big law firms. Despite the fact that Justin spent two years after law school in yeshivah, the firm hires him. We feel like Hashem is telling us: "You will never lose out by setting time aside to come to Israel and learn Torah." Once Justin gets the job, I feel better about our decision to move to LA. I still suffer from bouts of homesickness now and then, but Justin reassures me that living in New York is always on the table for us. This allows me to relax and embrace our time in California more.

In the months that follow, I take the California bar. As I await the results, I begin writing my story. And I can't stop. When I find out that I passed, I jump up and down, and then I continue writing.

It's clear to me that writing is part of my life purpose. I decide to pursue it. Law will always be there.

Slowly, we begin making friends in the community. As we host guests for Shabbos, I finally appreciate the amount of effort that goes into hosting. I call Ruthi and Illana and thank them for all the times they had me in their home.

Justin and I continue learning more about each other. As we experience the "growing pains" of *shanah rishonah*, I realize that marriage, like *avodas Hashem* (serving Hashem), is constant work. The main thing is that we are committed to each other, to this life, to building a *bayis ne'eman b'Yisrael*, a true Jewish home. Yes, being a *baal teshuvah* makes it more challenging at times, but really, we are all here to overcome challenges and fulfill our potential.

In 2018, three years after moving to LA, we are asked to speak at Rabbi Gradon's kollel dinner, a sign of how we have really become part of the community. The Pico-Robertson community is a special one, as Rabbi Gradon and other *rabbanim* make a special effort to support *baalei teshuvah*, people who have increased their Jewish observance and are trying to raise religious families in a healthy, grounded way.

We now have a little girl, Rachel Nechama, who is three years old. She has only begun her Jewish education, but she already knows who Hashem is, understands Shabbos, and can even say a few berachos (blessings)! She is named after my great-grandmother, Faigel Rochel, who always wanted to be more observant. I definitely sense that Rachel is an "old soul" who is comforted by Yiddishkeit. We get so much *nachas* from her, and from ourselves.

August 2020

Over the past year, Justin and I felt a strong pull back to Israel to pursue our dream of continued Torah learning. I am proud to say that we "took the jump," with Hashem's help, and moved to Israel (for now!). As I have learned, life is a journey and Hashem sends his messengers where He needs them. Thankfully, our families were very supportive, understanding that this is our dream. Their love for us is so strong that they were able to let us go, despite how it pains them for us to live so far away. We are beyond grateful and miss them every day.

Before we left for Israel, Rachel and I were outside looking at a tree, when we noticed a large branch. Rachel said, "Mommy, the branch is going to fly away."

"The branch won't fly away," I replied. "It's roots are very strong."

I immediately realized the deeper meaning behind my words. I've only been able to branch out as far as I have, and continue to do so, because my "roots," the unconditional love and support of Hashem and my family, are very strong, thank G-d.

And so, this is how a secular girl from the Five Towns became a *frum* wife and mother. I hope you have enjoyed hearing about my journey thus far as much as I have enjoyed sharing it. We should all be blessed to continue growing and fulfill our potential. Please be in touch; I would love to hear from you.

About the Author

JENNA MAIO ESQ. is a wife, mother, and freelance writer. She studied English and creative writing at Emory University and then completed a joint degree in law and environmental studies from the University of Pennsylvania Law School. Over the years, she learned at Neve Yerushalayim and Midreshet Rachel V'Chaya in Jerusalem, where she deepened her Jewish learning. She now hosts the Modern Jewish Girl podcast, available on Apple Podcasts and Spotify. She can be contacted through her website, www.modernjewishgirl.com.

This is her first book, adapted from the series "Princess Without a Crown," originally published in *Ami* magazine.